Manage Your Wealth Like a CEO

Manage Your Wealth Like a CEO

PERSONAL FINANCE
WITH A LEADERSHIP MINDSET

Chris Figaro, CFP®, CEPA®

CJF Books, LLC
Fitchburg, WI

Publisher's Cataloging-in-Publication Data

Figaro, Chris.
Manage your wealth like a CEO : personal finance with a leadership mindset / Chris Figaro – Fitchburg, WI : CJF Books, LLC, 2026.

p. ; cm.

ISBN13: 978-0-9601343-0-4 (paperback)
ISBN13: 978-0-9601343-1-1 (KDP)
ISBN13: 978-0-9601343-2-8 (ebook Kindle)
ISBN13: 978-0-9601343-3-5 (ebook Apple)

1. Finance, Personal. 2. Finance--Management. 3. Leadership.
HG179.F54 2026
332.024--dc23

Project coordination by Jenkins Group, Inc.
www.BookPublishing.com

Printed in the United States of America
30 29 28 27 26 • 5 4 3 2 1

DISCLOSURES

This book is provided for educational and informational purposes only. It is not intended to be, and should not be construed as, investment, tax, legal, or financial advice.

Nothing contained in this publication constitutes a recommendation to buy or sell any security, investment product, or strategy. All investments involve risk, including the possible loss of principal.

Hypothetical Examples and Assumptions

Any numerical examples, illustrations, rates of return, or assumptions are hypothetical and for illustrative purposes only. They do not represent actual performance and should not be relied upon for decision-making. All mathematical calculations, projections, and financial modeling are simplified for educational purposes and may not reflect the additional variables, compounding methods, tax implications, fees, and other factors present in actual financial situations.

Past performance, whether actual or hypothetical, is not indicative of future results. Investment returns, portfolio values, and withdrawal strategies are significantly affected by market volatility, sequence of returns, and the timing of withdrawals relative to market performance, particularly near retirement.

The hypothetical examples in this book feature individuals and families with specific income levels, tax brackets, family situations, and financial goals. Strategies that are appropriate for these hypothetical situations may not be suitable for readers with different circumstances, risk tolerances, time horizons, or financial objectives. No example should be considered a recommendation for any specific reader. Your situation will vary.

Tax and Legal Considerations

Tax laws, contribution limits, deduction thresholds, required minimum distribution ages, and other regulatory provisions referenced in this book are subject to change. The information provided reflects laws and limits in effect at the time of publication and may not reflect current requirements.

State and local laws, tax rates, creditor protection rules, estate laws, and insurance requirements vary significantly by jurisdiction. Examples and strategies discussed may not be applicable or optimal in all states.

Employer-Specific Plans and Benefits

Not all employer retirement plans offer the same features. Availability of Roth 401(k) options, after-tax contributions, in-service withdrawals, mega backdoor Roth conversions, NQDC plans, and employer matching programs varies by employer and plan. Readers should review their specific plan documents and consult with their plan administrator to understand available options.

Real Estate and Market Assumptions

Home price appreciation rates, rental inflation rates, and real estate market performance vary significantly by location, time period, and economic conditions. Historical averages do not guarantee future results. The rent vs. buy analysis includes assumptions about appreciation, rent inflation, and investment returns that are hypothetical and may not reflect actual market conditions in any specific area or time period.

Alternative Investments

Alternative investments involve additional risks, including illiquidity, lack of transparency, leverage, higher fees, and potential loss of principal. Some alternative investments may only be available to accredited investors. Alternative investment strategies may not be suitable for all investors and are not intended to be a complete investment program. It may be difficult to determine the current market value of the asset; and there may be limited historical risk and return data. Costs of purchase and sale may be relatively high. A high degree of investment analysis may be required before investing.

Insurance and Risk Management

Insurance needs, coverage amounts, policy types, and risk management strategies vary based on individual circumstances, state requirements, asset levels, and risk exposures. The insurance strategies discussed are examples only and should not be interpreted as recommendations for specific coverage types or amounts.

Professional Guidance Required

Many strategies discussed in this book require coordination among multiple professionals, including financial advisors, CPAs, estate attorneys, and insurance specialists. Implementing strategies without proper professional guidance and coordination may result in unintended tax consequences, legal issues, or financial losses. The "executive team" approach described is a framework, not a guarantee of outcomes. Readers should consult their own financial, tax, legal, and insurance professionals familiar with their specific circumstances and state regulations before making decisions.

Financial regulations, tax laws, investment products, and market conditions change over time. Readers should verify that information remains current and applicable before making financial decisions. The author does not have any obligation to update the information contained in this book.

Securities are offered through Steward Partners Investment Solutions, LLC ("SPIS"), registered broker/dealer, member FINRA/SIPC. Investment advisory services are offered through Steward Partners Investment Advisory, LLC ("SPIA"), an SEC-registered investment adviser. SPIS, SPIA, and Steward Partners Global Advisory, LLC are affiliates and collectively referred to as Steward Partners.

Chris Figaro is registered with and provides securities and/or advisory services through Steward Partners.

Steward Partners, its affiliates, and Steward Partners Wealth Managers do not provide tax or legal advice. You should consult with your tax advisor for matters involving taxation and tax planning and their attorney for matters involving trust and estate planning and other legal matters.

Certified Financial Planner Board of Standards Center for Financial Planning, Inc. owns and licenses the certification mark CFP® in the United States to Certified Financial Planner Board of Standards, Inc., which authorizes individuals who successfully complete the organization's initial and ongoing certification requirements to use the certification marks.

CONTENTS

INTRODUCTION

GROWING UP in New Jersey just south of New York City, I was always drawn to the idea of one day working on Wall Street. After college, the day finally came when I began my career as a trader on the American Stock Exchange.

Things were different on the AMEX, as they called it. Trading profits were made not by analyzing the fundamentals of a company but through technical dislocations in a company's implied volatility. It didn't matter how well or poorly a company operated; it was all about how volatile that stock or index traded on the open market.

As trading volume on the American Stock Exchange dwindled with the rise of electronic trading, I transitioned to Midtown Manhattan to work alongside some of the best and brightest in the hedge fund world. It was there where I learned what really drives growth—buying fundamentally sound companies. Investing in a business with a strong balance sheet, solid free cash flow, and sound risk management became the foundation for identifying long-term growth opportunities.

Eventually, I left New York City and moved to Wisconsin, where I transitioned from institutional money management to retail wealth management. After almost 10 years at a large financial institution, my business partners and I started our wealth management firm, Vantage Point Private Wealth.

Having a background in financial markets and analyzing companies with portfolio managers laid the foundation for how I think about managing wealth for clients today. There is a clear similarity between sound financial companies and families who take control of their wealth.

When most people hear the words "wealth management," they think of investing in stocks, bonds, and mutual funds. That's the default. But investing is only part of the story. If that's all you focus on, you're flying blind to the bigger picture.

This book is designed to help you think differently, to approach your financial life the way a CEO thinks about running a successful business—one with leadership, defined strategy and team collaboration. Managing wealth isn't just about picking the right investments; it's about understanding how all the moving parts (your assets, liabilities, cash flow, goals, taxes, risks, and legacy) work together. Throughout the book I will make comparisons between managing a successful company and managing wealth.

Wealth management comes down to five core areas. I'll walk you through each of them throughout this book. They're not complicated but often ignored by those who think building wealth lives only in a brokerage account.

Here's a quick look at the five key wealth management areas and their similarities to managing a company:

Asset and Liability Management
(Balance Sheet Management)

This is the process of managing your assets (stocks, bonds, cash, homes, cars, clothes) and liabilities (mortgage, credit cards, car loans, securitized loans, etc.) in the most efficient way. A successful company is one that can efficiently manage its business assets (fixed and operational) with the potential use of the right amount of leverage if warranted.

Short-Term Cash Flow Management
(Cash Flow Management)

This is the process of managing the inflow of cash (from a paycheck, Social Security, sale of vested company stock, sale of a private stock, inheritance, etc.) to either personal assets (lifestyle assets) or investment assets (assets that will be sold at a later date to subsidize the lack of cash inflow). A successful company is one that can strategically manage its cash flow (revenue from services provided or goods sold) into either fixed or operational assets.

Long-Term Goal Planning
(Business Strategy)

This is the process of ultimately deciding what you want out of your wealth. (Retirement at 55? Two homes? A legacy for kids and grandkids?) Yogi Berra stated, "If you don't know where you are going, you will end up someplace else." A successful business is one that has goals and a vision to move toward.

Risk and Tax Management
(Insurance and Tax Planning)

This is the process of running all of the above in the most tax-efficient way while protecting all that you have built. A successful company understands the tax code and has a plan in place to protect all that it has created.

Legacy Planning
(Succession Planning)

This is the process of passing on all that you have built in your lifetime in a way that you want (not a way the state in which you reside wants). It is important to always have this in place regardless of age; however, the complexity grows over time with your wealth and family size. A successful business is one that always has a succession plan for its key executives in the event of death, disability, or departure of the company.

These five areas work together. And when one is missing or ignored, the whole plan could break down. That's the problem I see most often in wealth management: not lack of effort but lack of coordination. Most focus on investing without stepping back, to see how all the parts fit together. These five areas give you a framework for making smarter decisions, reducing blind spots, and building something that lasts.

The final part of this book focuses on how to turn this framework into action. You'll learn how to assemble your personal "executive team": financial advisor, CPA, estate attorney, and other specialists who work for you, not just with you. Professionals who understand the big picture and can help build a plan that actually gets implemented and not just talked about.

This book is here to help you think more strategically, take control of your financial life, and build something that's aligned with your goals and intentions—the way a CEO runs a company.

Let's get started.

CHAPTER 1

WHAT IS A CHIEF EXECUTIVE OFFICER (CEO)?

"Great things in business are never done by one person. They're done by a team of people." —Steve Jobs

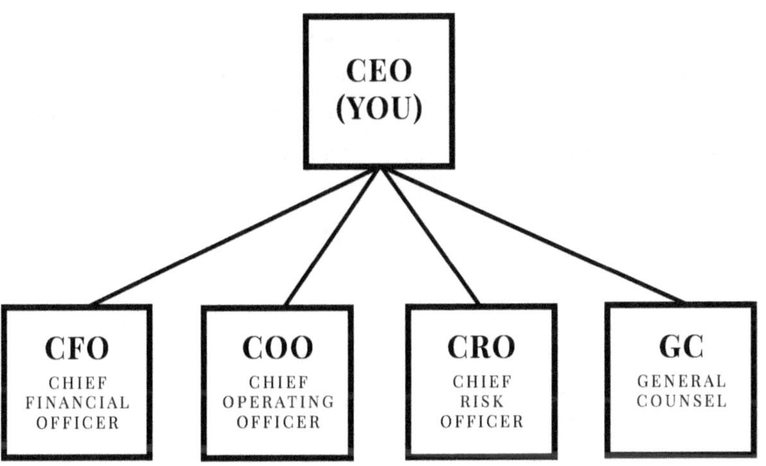

You Are the CEO of Your Wealth

IN THE CORPORATE WORLD, the chief executive officer (CEO) is the highest-ranking leader in an organization. This person is responsible for setting the company's vision, creating strategy, and building the team needed to bring that vision to life. A strong CEO does not need to master every function in the business, but they must understand the big picture and make smart decisions with the help of experts.

In your personal financial life, you hold that same position. You are the CEO of your wealth. Whether you are building your career, managing a growing family, or preparing for retirement, your financial decisions shape your future. You are not just earning and spending; you are leading. And like any good CEO, your success depends on surrounding yourself with the right team of experts who can help you grow and protect what you have built.

Too many people try to manage wealth without a clear structure. They work with a CPA for taxes, an insurance agent for protection, and a financial advisor for investments, but no one is talking to each other. There is no strategy. No unified direction. That is like running a company where departments do not meet, goals are not aligned, and the team lacks leadership. That is where your role as the CEO becomes essential.

Let's look at the key executives on a typical corporate leadership team and how they relate to the professionals who should support your personal wealth.

CHAPTER 2
YOUR KEY "EXECUTIVES"

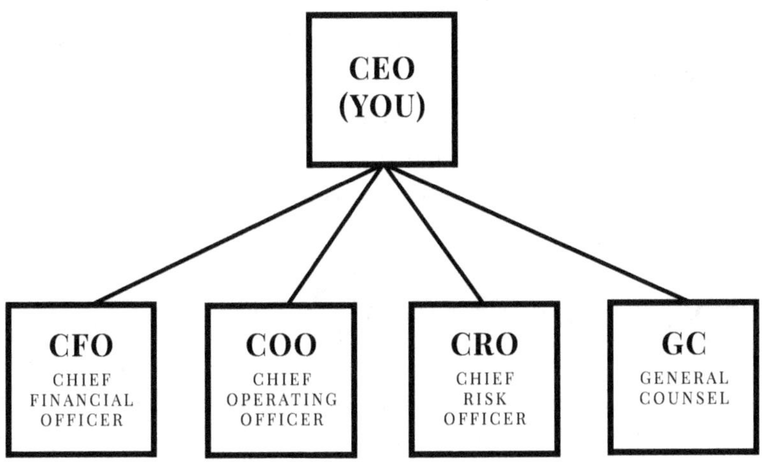

YOUR KEY EXECUTIVES:

CFO=Financial Advisor and CPA
COO=Financial Advisor
CRO=Insurance Agent
GC=Estate and Business Attorney

Chief Financial Officer (CFO)

Your Financial Advisor and Accountant

The CFO is responsible for managing a company's financial health. They track revenue and expenses, oversee financial reporting, manage the company's balance sheet and cash flow statements, and ensure that resources are being used wisely. Their job is to create financial clarity so the CEO can make informed decisions and see a clear path into the future.

In your personal financial life, this role is often filled by your financial advisor and accountant. A trustworthy accountant and financial advisor team helps you understand your income and expenses, monitors your net worth, and helps build a financial strategy that matches your future goals. This team brings insight and objectivity so you can lead your financial life with confidence and clarity.

An experienced financial advisor and accountant team brings a defined strategy to the table. They look for ways to lower your tax burden, increase your efficiency, and coordinate your tax strategy with your overall financial plan. This includes planning around capital gains, income timing, charitable giving, and other tools that can improve your overall wealth management plan.

Chief Operating Officer (COO)

Your Financial Advisor

The COO turns strategy into action. They make sure that the company runs efficiently and that the organization is moving forward in line with the CEO's vision. They coordinate across departments, solve problems, and help make strategy real by bringing it all together into one unified plan to move forward.

In your personal life, your financial advisor plays this role by implementing all the various components that make up a financial plan. They help you set up investment asset accounts, validate that the right assets are in the right places, and coordinate with all of your other advisors to help ensure that your entire financial system is aligned with your goals and is functioning smoothly.

Chief Risk Officer (CRO)

Your Insurance Agent

The CRO identifies and manages potential risks to the business. That might include financial risk, legal risk, or operational risk. Their role is to help prevent unexpected losses and protect the company from events that could cause harm.

In your personal life, this function is handled most of the time by your insurance agent. Their job is to protect all that you have built from unexpected threats. This could mean life insurance to protect your family; disability coverage to protect your income; and auto, home, and umbrella insurance to safeguard your car, home, and overall assets, respectively. They help put the right protections in place so that you are not vulnerable to the unpredictable.

General Counsel

Your Estate Planning and Business Attorney

Every business needs legal oversight, and that is the responsibility of the general counsel. They help ensure that the company is operating within the law, and they assist with contracts, compliance, and the legal complexities of planning for potential transitions.

In your financial life, this role is filled by your estate planning or business attorney. They help you create legal documents that protect your family, clarify your wishes now and upon passing, and ensure that your assets are handled according to your values. This includes wills, trusts, powers of attorney, and other legal tools that provide structure and security for your wealth.

Board of Directors

Your Family and Trusted Voices

Even the most talented CEO needs a sounding board. A board of directors provides perspective, oversight, and accountability. They challenge assumptions, offer guidance, and help the CEO stay true to the mission.

In your personal life, this role may be filled by your various family members, adult children, close friends, business partners, or close mentors. These are the people whose opinions matter to you and who are affected by your financial decisions. Involving them in the planning process where appropriate can lead to better outcomes and stronger alignment with your values.

CHAPTER 3

ASSET AND LIABILITY MANAGEMENT

"Never invest in a company without understanding its finances. The biggest losses in stocks come from companies with poor balance sheets." —Peter Lynch

IT'S TIME to dive into the Five Pillars of Wealth Management and how to approach them like a CEO. The first pillar is *asset and liability management (balance sheet management).*

In their simplest form, assets and liabilities represent what you own and what you owe. They're recorded on a balance sheet, which serves as the foundation of your wealth management plan.

An asset is essentially anything that you own that holds some sort of value. Your assets are either tangible (can be touched) or intangible (cannot be touched). Here are a few examples of each:

Tangible Assets

Your car, primary and/or secondary home, furniture, jewelry, computer, clothes—essentially anything that has been purchased and has physical form.

Intangible Assets

The equity, fixed income, cash, and alternative investments in your 401(k) or brokerage accounts. This also includes trademarks, copyrights, and even your meaningful experiences from a vacation.

"Tangible" and "intangible" describe whether an asset can be physically held. While important, the main driver, however, is what an asset can actually do for you once purchased. Assets typically fall into two main categories:

Personal Assets

An asset you purchase for personal use or enjoyment. They help you get through each day in a more comfortable, efficient, or potentially meaningful way.

Investment Assets

An asset you purchase with the intention of selling it or giving it away in the future at a higher value than what you originally paid. These assets are the main driver of wealth and will help you "retire" in the future.

Understanding the difference between these two types of assets is crucial. It forms the basis for knowing how your assets can support both your life now and your future. We will explore each of them further in the next section.

Liabilities, on the other hand, represent what you owe. A liability is created when you borrow money and have a legal obligation to pay it back with interest over a set period of time. Think of a mortgage as a common example.

Liabilities also fall into two categories: those that can help grow your wealth and those that work against your wealth—in simple terms, good liabilities and bad liabilities.

Good Liabilities

Mortgages, securitized loans with favorable interest rates, student loans when used to improve long-term earning potential.

Bad Liabilities

Credit card debt, auto loans, high-interest personal loans, or other forms of expensive debt.

Whether a liability is good or bad depends on several factors. The most important are the terms of the loan, the interest rate, and the type of asset being purchased with the borrowed money. It can get confusing, and we'll break it down in more detail later.

In a business, the balance sheet is one of the most important tools a CEO uses to understand the company's financial health. It provides a clear picture of what the business owns (its assets) and what it owes (its liabilities). The difference between the two is the company's equity, or book value. A strong balance sheet allows the business to navigate uncertainty, reinvest in itself, and create long-term value. A weak one can limit flexibility and increase financial pressure. When your balance sheet is well managed, you have the ability to stay on your toes during uncertain times while others are on their heels.

Just like your personal balance sheet, business assets typically fall into two main categories: fixed assets and operating assets. Fixed assets are long term in nature and designed to support the business. These can include the company's real estate (just like you need a home to live in) and equipment (just like you need a car to get around or furniture in your home). Operating assets, on the other hand, are intended to be purchased and sold to generate a profit. These might include cash reserves or long-term investments (just like you hold opportunistic cash or investment assets to generate interest or grow your portfolio) and inventory (similar to buying equity with the intent to sell it later at a higher price). Operating assets are what drive revenue and growth for the company.

Liabilities (debt) also play a role in business strategy and can be categorized as good and bad liabilities. A CEO might use debt to fund expansion, invest in new technology, or acquire a competitor, which in turn could be a good liability if there is growth on the asset purchased. However, when taken on without a plan, entailing a high interest rate, or being used to purchase a fixed asset that does not generate profit, they can lead to cash flow problems and added risk.

As an individual, you may not think of your balance sheet in this way. But by managing your balance sheet (assets and liabilities) like a CEO and applying the same principles, you gain a clearer view of your financial position and the path forward.

Let's take a closer look at each part.

ASSET OVERVIEW

As stated above, an asset is anything you own that holds some form of value. This can include everything from the house you live in (if purchased and not rented) and the equity holdings in your brokerage account to the pen sitting on your desk. All of these assets were acquired using either cash or debt, and each purchase made consciously or unconsciously was a decision rooted in either personal use or investment intent.

Assets are categorized as either tangible (physical and touchable) or intangible (nonphysical). While that distinction matters, the more important question is *what the asset can actually do for you once it's owned.* Understanding the role each asset plays in your life is where thinking like a CEO can help you build wealth over time.

Personal Assets
(similar to fixed assets in a business)

These are assets purchased for personal use or enjoyment. They help you get through daily life in a more comfortable, efficient, or meaningful way.

Investment Assets
(similar to operating assets in a business)

These are assets purchased with the intent to grow in value over time, either to be sold or to be passed down as part of your legacy. Investment assets are the primary driver of long-term wealth and are what ultimately allow you to retire or reach financial independence.

Let's explore how each of these plays a key role in balance sheet management, starting with personal assets.

PERSONAL ASSETS

Personal assets are the essentials that keep your life running smoothly and bring satisfaction along the way. Often referred to as lifestyle assets, they can be tangible or intangible, but they're typically not intended to be sold later to support retirement or fund long-term financial goals.

Every purchase, big or small, plays a role in your overall financial picture. These assets represent the *wants and needs* that maintain your lifestyle and usually remain in the personal asset bucket.

Personal assets are similar to fixed assets in a business. Fixed assets are the resources a company needs to operate: office building, desks, computers, cash registers, even the pool table in the employee lounge. These aren't bought to turn a profit; they are acquired through thoughtful analysis to ensure that the cost makes sense. They're the tools that support daily operations of the business.

Just like a CEO decides how much capital to allocate toward fixed assets while preserving enough for revenue-generating investments, you must decide how much of your resources to put into personal assets without jeopardizing your future wealth-building potential.

Here's how personal assets compare to fixed assets in a business:

- Personal assets of your household = fixed assets of a business
- Your personal home = a company headquarters
- Your dining table, stools, laptop, car, or personal plane = a company's furniture, tech, vehicles, or company plane
- The more you spend on personal assets, the less there is for investment assets = the more a CEO spends on fixed assets, the less there is for growth-producing assets

Let's take a closer look at some common personal assets on your balance sheet, how they show up in your daily life, and the impact they have on your broader financial picture. For most people, the most significant personal asset is their primary home. Everyone needs a place to live, whether purchased or rented. Renting means that you avoid depleting your investment assets for a down payment. Buying, on the other hand, typically requires you to shift a portion of your investment assets into a personal asset—the home—which often remains in that category forever.

Owning or renting a home involves more than just finding a place to live; it's a financial decision that can affect your long-term wealth in many ways. A home is often your largest personal asset, and the choice between renting or owning directly affects both your lifestyle and your balance sheet. Each option comes with trade-offs, and we'll explore how both impact your personal and investment assets over time.

Let's assume that you are weighing the option of buying a $1,000,000 home or renting a home for $5,000 per month. You have managed to save $200,000 of taxable investment assets as a potential down payment. These assets have been saved over the years outside of your 401(k) and are currently held as investment assets in a brokerage account (discussed more in the next section).

If you choose to rent, the analysis is pretty simple. The total cost over the lifetime of the rental can be figured out by multiplying your rent by duration and adding in a yearly inflation cost. This is purely an expense and builds zero equity over time. The two monetary investment asset add-backs are the growth of the down payment (that would have been used to purchase the home) AND, if the monthly rental cost is lower than the total monthly cost of owning a home, that dollar value can be transitioned into your investment assets for growth.

A summary of things to consider when renting a home:

- You will not have to use your investment assets as a down payment, and the $200,000 as mentioned above can continue to stay invested.
- If the monthly cost of the rental is less than the total monthly cost of owning the home (mortgage, taxes, miscellaneous items of home ownership), that value can be outflowed to investment assets.
- For this example, let's assume that the rental cost of $5,000 covers everything to live in the home and for simplicity's sake no inflation is considered.

If you choose to buy, the inputs become a bit more involved. Purchasing a home typically requires a down payment pulled from your investment assets and a liability in the form of a mortgage. That loan comes with costs tied to the interest rate and length of the mortgage. Homeownership also includes additional ongoing expenses which tend to inflate over time, but it may offer some tax benefits through mortgage interest deductions. Unlike renting, a portion of your monthly payment goes toward building equity in the home as the mortgage is paid down, which can help you build long-term lifestyle wealth.

A summary of things to consider when buying a home using the example above:

- The total cost of the home would be a $200,000 down payment, the 30-year fixed mortgage of $800,000 at 6% and the annual costs to run the house such as maintenance, taxes and insurance.
- The total monthly cost to own, for simplicity's sake, is $4,800 as the mortgage payment and $2,700 to cover yearly maintenance, taxes and insurance that do not inflate, totaling $7,500 per month.
- The equity that you build typically stays in the personal asset bucket and is usually not a source of capital for living down the road when income stops.

Let's look at the numbers a little more closely to give you an idea of how to analyze home ownership versus renting.

Financial considerations[1] to think about when either buying or renting a home using the information given:

- Potential down payment (how much you are willing to initially invest in a new home so that it does not affect your overall liquidity): $200,000
- Monthly ownership cost of the home versus monthly rent with inflation: $7,500 versus $5,000
- Current interest rates to determine cost of mortgage: 6% on a 30-year mortgage
- Future growth rate on investments assets: ~8%
- Future growth rate on your personal home: ~4%

[1] Mortgage interest rate, investment return, and home appreciation assumptions used are hypothetical, provided for illustrative purposes only, and actual results may differ due to market conditions, economic factors, and other variables

A hypothetical example of your living situation over a 30-year time frame as a renter:

1. **Rent cost over time:**
   - $5,000 x 12 months x 30 years: ~$1,800,000 cost of rent (Yikes!)
2. **Invested monthly cash flow based on the difference between paying $5,000 per month versus $7,500:**
   - This equates to about a $900,000 outflow to investment assets, which results in roughly $3,400,000 after a 30-year time frame
3. **Growth of down payment of $200,000 not used:**
   - $200,000 invested at 8% per year over a 30-year time frame: ~$2,000,000
4. **To sum up the rental cash flow:**
   - $1,800,000 sunk cost to personal rent expense (never getting this back)
   - $900,000 outflow to investments from lower rent versus own cost over 30 years (investment asset)
   - $200,000 stays in investment assets since not purchasing a home (investment asset)
   - Total outflow of $2,900,000
5. **To sum up the ending value of renting:**
   - ~$2,000,000 is the ending value of the down payment not used
   - ~$3,400,000 is the ending value of the monthly savings rate of the excess cash flow from the lower monthly cost over 30 years
   - At the end of 30 years you are left with 0 in personal assets (still do not own a home) and roughly $5,400,000 in investment assets

The owning part of the equation is a bit more complex. The total cost of owning a home is the cost of the home, the cost of the liability to purchase the home (if you do not pay all cash for it), annual property taxes, and the miscellaneous items to maintain the house. An added benefit that homeownership provides is the potential to deduct a portion of your mortgage interest and property taxes if the combined is greater than your standard deduction when filing your taxes. Home ownership builds personal asset equity.

A hypothetical example of your living situation over a 30-year time frame as a buyer:

- **Purchase cost over time:**
  - $7500 x 12 months x 30 years = $2,700,000 + $200,000 down payment $2,900,000 (same cash flow from renting, just allocated differently)
- **At the end of 30 years:**
  - A house worth roughly $3,200,000, if assuming an annual growth rate of 4%

This is a very broad overview of renting versus owning, and there are other qualitative and quantitative things to consider during the process. This hypothetical was a simple illustration of things to consider when thinking about the rent versus buy scenario. Even if the numbers support renting over buying, there are important nonfinancial factors to weigh. For example, rent prices rarely go down, and while you may enjoy a stable lease for a few years, you have little control over what happens next. Annual rent increases can outpace inflation, especially in high-demand areas, and there's always the risk of your landlord choosing not to renew your lease, or the property can be sold while you are a tenant. This lack of control can add a layer of uncertainty to your financial planning. Owning a home, on the other hand, typically comes with a fixed mortgage payment (if you opt for a fixed-rate loan), which can offer more predictability in your long-term housing costs. However, there are additional variable costs to consider as an owner such as annual maintenance, taxes and insurance which also tend to inflate over time.

Renting offers a level of flexibility that homeownership simply can't match. If you're not committed to a specific location or if your career has you in a location for only a short period of time, renting allows you to adapt without the financial and logistical burdens of selling a home. It's a great way to test out a neighborhood or city before fully committing, especially if you're considering a relocation for work or retirement. Renting also removes many of the responsibilities tied to ownership. You're not on the hook for major repairs, property taxes, or ongoing maintenance costs like a new roof, HVAC issues, or landscaping. That freedom can reduce stress, preserve liquidity, and allow you to redirect capital toward other investment opportunities.

Your primary residence is often one of the largest personal assets on your balance sheet. Whether you rent or own, it deserves thoughtful analysis. The decision isn't just about what you can afford; it's about what supports your broader financial strategy, lifestyle goals, and long-term flexibility.

Another essential personal asset for many people, especially those living in suburban areas, is a car. For families, this might mean owning two or more vehicles. Once a car is purchased, whether using cash flow or investment assets, it becomes a personal asset and typically stays in that category until it's traded in or sold.

Cars are relatively straightforward when it comes to cost. You pay the full sticker price upfront, lease (which is similar to renting), or finance the purchase by combining a down payment with a loan. If you have the liquidity, you should pay the $40,000, for example, from your investment assets. In that case, the cost of the car is simple: *$40,000 plus any associated fees.*

Over time, the value of the car will depreciate depending on how long you own it. The loss in value represents the cost of ownership.

If you don't have $40,000 available in investment assets, a common option is to use part investment assets and part loan (bad liability). For example, using the $40,000 sticker price above, you may choose to put $10,000 down and finance the remaining $30,000 with a loan. While the depreciation is the same, this route comes with the added cost of interest on the $30,000 loan. In this case, your total car cost could look like the following: *$10,000 down payment + fees at purchase + $30,000 loan paydown + interest on loan*. I will explain later why this type of loan is categorized as a bad liability.

The final option is leasing. Leasing typically requires less money upfront and spreads the cost over monthly payments for a fixed term, usually around three years. The monthly payment represents the difference between the car's purchase price and its residual value at the end of the lease, plus fees and interest. In both a lease and a financed purchase, you're paying extra for the use of borrowed capital. Only an outright purchase avoids that added cost, but it also requires significantly more liquidity upfront.

Another important personal asset is your emergency fund. Your emergency fund is a cash reserve on your balance sheet intended to provide financial stability in case of unexpected events. It is designed to cover unforeseen expenses related to your personal assets. For example, if your furnace breaks down, if you need new tires for your car, or if you lose your job, your emergency fund should ideally cover your expenses for about six months. A job loss, which is often unpredictable and typically lasts less than a year, should be managed using your emergency fund rather than tapping into investment assets, which are meant for long-term goals. An emergency fund is typically set to a specific amount and remains stable, even during retirement. This personal asset provides liquidity during times of need and offers peace of mind, knowing that if something disrupts your cash flow, you have the resources to cover your monthly expenses for a period of time.

As I've mentioned before, personal assets are similar to fixed assets in a business. When purchased, they require a CEO to strategize with the leadership team to ensure that the company allocates capital in the most efficient way. For example, deciding whether to lease or purchase a corporate headquarters is a major conversation, as is a purchase or renting of a home. At certain points in the business lifecycle, the company might even sell its building to unlock equity and then lease it back, a strategy known as a sale-leaseback. This move is often driven by the company's financial needs or shifts in the macroeconomic environment.

A business also needs to decide how many vehicles to provide for its sales team and which perks are necessary to support the desired workplace culture. Just like managing fixed assets, a company must also keep a close eye on its cash position to ensure that it maintains enough liquidity to weather potential revenue downturns, similar to how you manage your emergency fund.

Key questions to think about regarding your personal assets:

- Should you purchase or rent a home—what makes the most sense given your current balance sheet, current and future economic conditions, cash flow, and long-term goals?
- Should you buy a car or lease it?
- How much excess cash should you have for unforeseen liquidity needs?
- Are the things that you buy on a monthly basis wants or needs, and if they are wants, are they worth the opportunity cost of not redirecting those funds to investment assets?

Overview of Personal Assets

Personal assets are lifestyle assets. They are the wants and needs that help you get through the day and help make your life operational and potentially more enjoyable. Unfortunately, they will not help you retire sooner or build long-term wealth, as most personal assets are depreciating assets outside of your home. It is up to you how much to spend on these items, as anything leftover will spill into investment assets, the generator of long-term wealth.

Similar to personal assets on your balance sheet, a CEO needs to purchase non-revenue-generating fixed assets so the company can operate.

Fixed assets, just like personal assets, are the foundation of the company and help the business operate on a day-to-day basis.

Personal asset examples:

- Home (or second home or third home) and everything in it
- Car
- Boat
- Clothes
- Emergency fund
- The stuff on the upper shelves in your closet and garage
- The experience of a vacation
- The assets on your personal balance sheet that provide or have provided for a desired lifestyle

Fixed asset examples as they relate to a business:

- Company HQ
- Company cars
- Corporate travel
- Desks, chairs, computers for employees
- The asset within a company that is purchased to form the foundation of the company

INVESTMENT ASSETS

You should now have a better understanding of personal assets. Investment assets are purchased with cash that is left over after your personal assets are purchased; they are your "savings." Investment assets are purchased with the main goal of generating income or growth over time so that one day you can either spend them on a personal asset in retirement (when you no longer have a paycheck) or give them away as defined in your legacy. Typically, these purchases are equity, fixed income, nonemergency cash, or alternative investments. These are the assets that are considered "savings." They are the assets that will one day hopefully supplement your income when you stop working. If you spend every dollar on personal assets and save nothing, you would either have to work your whole life and use the cash flow from a salary, for example, to pay for your personal assets (assuming you do not inherit money) or depend on the government through Social Security.

Investment assets are like the operational assets of a business. Operational assets are the assets that are purchased that will typically generate revenue for a company—it's why the company exists. It could be the ingredients purchased to make the final product of a beverage or food item, for example. It could be the inventory of parts that make the completed car ready for sale. These assets are investments that are purchased that in turn will be sold as a whole to create revenue. The more a company has from cash flow to buy operating assets, the more product the company can make, which in turn becomes revenue/profits.

Here's how investment assets compare to operational assets in a business:

- Investment assets of your household = operational assets of a business.
- The purchase of an equity fund in your 401(k) that will one day be used to supplement your income in retirement = the purchase of inventory to create a product to sell.
- The more you purchase in investment assets, the less dependent you are on a paycheck in the future = the more a CEO uses for the purchase of operational assets, the more revenue and potentially profit the company will make.

When you receive income, you can choose to buy a personal asset or "save" into the investment bucket with an investment asset. If you are not buying clothes or a new car or adding a pool, then what do you buy? The investment assets that you can purchase are *equities, fixed income, nonemergency cash*, and *alternative investments*, which are held with the goal of long-term growth and income generation. Without going into too much detail, I will explain each on a high level.

Equity represents ownership. When you purchase equity, you're buying a piece of a company and gain access to its future growth and potential cash flows. This might look like buying a few shares of a specific company or investing in a broader stock index fund through your 401(k). Equities tend to offer the highest potential for long-term growth, but they also come with more risk and short-term volatility. You can access equities through individual stocks, exchange-traded funds (ETFs), and mutual funds.

Fixed income is the opposite of ownership; it's lending. When you invest in fixed income, you're essentially loaning money to a company or government entity in exchange for periodic interest payments and the return of your principal at the end of the term. These investments are generally more conservative and are used to provide income and stability for a portfolio. Fixed-income options include government bonds, corporate bonds, or fixed-income mutual funds and ETFs.

Cash and cash equivalents represent the most liquid and stable asset class, though they typically offer the lowest returns. These include savings accounts, money market funds, and short-term treasury bills. It's important to distinguish between operational cash, which is used for monthly living expenses, and nonemergency cash, which is cash set aside to be invested in the future. While nonemergency cash may earn some interest, it's mainly held for flexibility and short-term safety rather than growth. Its low risk also means it's unlikely to keep up with inflation over time, which limits its long-term utility.

Alternative investments are assets that fall outside of the traditional stock and bond markets. These include private equity, private credit, real estate, infrastructure, commodities, hedge funds, and even digital assets like cryptocurrency. Unlike publicly traded investments, alternatives are not bought and sold on standard exchanges; you can't just click a button to own a share of a private company or a piece of a real estate deal. They often require higher minimum investments, carry higher risk, and may be available only to accredited investors through a financial advisor or institution. While less accessible, alternatives can offer diversification and the opportunity to tap into areas of the investment world that don't move in lockstep with the public markets.

The four investment asset classes above are typically purchased with excess cash that remains after your lifestyle needs (personal assets) have been met. As the CEO of your wealth, think of this as your retained earnings, the portion of your cash flow that isn't consumed by monthly costs (fixed assets) and can instead be reinvested for future growth (operational assets). These investment assets are acquired with a single intention: to build long-term wealth that can support you later in life, especially during the stage when you are no longer actively earning income from your career or business.

Over time, the goal for these assets is to appreciate in value, generate income, or both. Ideally, they appreciate enough to not only preserve your lifestyle but replace your dependent monthly income entirely. In some cases they can provide ongoing cash flow without requiring you to sell any portion of the asset. For example, if you have a $5,000,000 portfolio of equities, fixed income, and alternatives that yield 3.5% between all of the asset classes, that will create an annual income stream of $175,000 without needing to sell any portion of the asset.

During the wealth accumulation phase of your life, one of the most important skills to master is balancing cash flow—**the Balancing Act**, which is a concept we'll explore in more detail later. Managing this balance effectively is what allows you to consistently build your investment assets over time. It's the four investment asset classes that will ultimately fund a future lifestyle that's financially independent and on your terms.

As you approach your wealth like a CEO, it becomes clear that building long-term wealth requires a deliberate plan that prioritizes saving into investment assets while still leaving room to enjoy life. The real challenge is balancing planning for tomorrow (investment assets fund this lifestyle) while enjoying the present (personal assets fund this lifestyle). It's one of the most strategic decisions you'll make as the CEO of your wealth.

Overview of Investment Assets

Unlike personal assets (lifestyle assets), investment assets are the assets that will supplement your income when you no longer are receiving an income from your employment or business. The more you can direct cash flow (discussed later) into these assets (save), the sooner you can stop depending on employment or a paycheck to supplement your income.

Similar to investment assets on your balance sheet, a CEO of a business needs to strategically invest in the assets that will generate revenue for the company. Operational assets are similar to your investment assets, as they are purchased to eventually sell at a higher value to create revenue that will ultimately cycle back into fixed assets or more operational assets.

Investment asset examples:

- Equities (single companies or an ETF)
- Fixed income (government or corporate bonds)
- Nonemergency cash (stable asset that can later be used for other investment assets)
- Alternative investments (private equity, private real estate, private credit, hedge funds, digital assets, commodities)
- The asset on your balance sheet that is intended to be purchased so that it will grow in value and provide cash inflow in the future

Operational asset examples:

- The business inventory to create a final product

- Marketing and branding to create a larger customer base
- A piece of real estate with the intent to sell at a later date or to rent out for income
- The asset within a company that is purchased to create future revenue for the company

THE BALANCING ACT

You should now understand the two main types of assets on your balance sheet: personal assets (your lifestyle assets) and investment assets (your savings and wealth-building assets). We'll dive into cash flow next, but it's important to recognize that when cash flows into your operational account, you have a choice to spend it on personal assets or direct it toward investment assets. How you choose to reallocate your cash inflow to cash outflow is what I call **the Balancing Act**.

PERSONAL ASSETS **INVESTMENT ASSETS**

PERSONAL ASSETS:

WANTS AND NEEDS / LIFESTYLE ASSETS
EQUAL TO FIXED ASSETS IN A BUSINESS

INVESTMENT ASSETS:

SAVINGS / WEALTH BUILDING ASSETS
EQUAL TO OPERATING ASSETS IN A BUSINESS

To illustrate this, let's look at two very different individuals: the **Super Saver** and the **Super Spender**.

The Super Saver earns $200,000 a year, which after taxes leaves about $150,000 of take-home income (cash inflow). Her goal is to maximize her investment assets while keeping personal asset expenses to a minimum so she can "retire" as soon as possible. She lives in a modest home, drives a basic car, takes an occasional vacation, and hunts for value in every purchase. She maxes out her 401(k) and allocates what's left over from personal asset spending to her investment assets (equities, fixed income, alternative investments, and opportunistic cash). Because of this discipline, the Super Saver is able to retire comfortably after just 20 years, living fully off the wealth she has built in her investment accounts. She no longer depends on employment income and can enjoy life on her terms.

The Super Spender, on the other hand, earns $300,000 a year, about $225,000 after taxes. His focus is on living life to the fullest now. He takes multiple vacations, lives in a large home that is mortgaged 90%, and has two cars and a boat. While he enjoys a high-quality lifestyle today, very little of his income is left to build investment assets. Aside from a minimal 401(k) contribution and a couple hundred extra dollars a month, almost nothing is saved. After 30 years of working, he still has the house, the memories, and the car payments (these usually never stop, unfortunately) but very few investment assets. As a result, he remains dependent on his paycheck and cannot rely on Social Security alone to cover his personal asset expenses in retirement. Without accumulated investment assets to subsidize his future lifestyle, the only option is to keep working and trading time for money while delaying financial freedom.

Just like a CEO, managing your personal balance sheet should be intentional and strategic. Having a clear plan, with input from your financial "executive team," can help you decide how much to allocate to investment assets and personal assets each year. This decision directly impacts when you can realistically stop relying on employment income and shift to living off your wealth.

Some might argue that the Super Saver isn't fully enjoying life today because she's directing most of her income toward investments instead of experiences, skipping big vacations or recreational assets. On the other hand, the Super Spender is maximizing enjoyment now, but eventually, he may want to stop trading his time for money and rely more on investment assets. The challenge for the Super Spender? That lifestyle shift requires planning and a runway of time to build wealth.

The ideal approach for most people lies somewhere in between. You want to enjoy life now with meaningful experiences and purchases while still being conscious about saving and building your investment assets. That balance is what leads to long-term financial freedom.

With that foundation in place, let's now look at the *liability side* of your balance sheet. This is the money you borrow (debt) to afford larger purchases now that can't be paid for in full immediately with your cash flow.

LIABILITY OVERVIEW

Assets are what you *own*; a liability (debt) is what you *owe*. We will now discuss the use of debt to pay for an asset versus exchanging cash.

There are two main reasons you will use debt:

1. You do not have enough cash to cover the full cost of an asset.
2. You believe that the rate at which you borrow (interest rate) will be less than the growth rate of the asset you purchase or another like asset.

The process of getting a loan is simple: you borrow money, you pay interest on the amount borrowed, and you pay back the full amount borrowed over a particular time. The key terms are the duration of the loan, the interest rate at which you borrow, and the asset that you intend to purchase with the borrowed funds. This ultimately determines whether the liability is good or bad.

GOOD LIABILITIES

Good liabilities are typically used to purchase assets that are designed to generate income or appreciate over time. They're strategic by nature and can contribute to long-term financial growth when used correctly. In most cases, good liabilities are tied to your investment assets, not your personal assets (except for your home). If the asset purchased with debt has the potential to grow in value or produce income, using debt to acquire it can make sense as long as the terms of the liability support the overall financial outcome. The defining trait of a good liability is its ability to help create wealth, not destroy it.

A good liability is one that has a relatively low interest rate, with a longer term, and is being used to purchase a tangible asset (real estate, for example) or intangible asset (equity or education, for example) that will grow in value (appreciate) over time at a greater rate than the interest that is being paid on the loan.

That is really all you need to know about debt. Every time you are thinking about buying a particular asset, whether personal or investment, ask yourself two questions:

1. Do I have the cash now to buy the asset without the use of debt?
2. Will the value of the asset I am purchasing grow at a rate greater than the interest I am paying?

Most of the time people will use debt in the form of credit cards, car loans, and boat loans because they do not have the cash on hand to purchase the personal asset presently and have to use future cash flow to pay for it. If the asset that is being purchased loses value over time (depreciates) and you do not have the cash to pay for it all now, the purchase really needs to be evaluated further to determine whether it is truly a need or just a want. The truth is that the asset that you are purchasing will cost you even more than the listed price since you are paying interest on top of the cost. That is typically why using debt for anything other than a strategic purchase does not make sense unless it is an essential personal asset.

Think about the dynamics of this particular example: A bank lent a family $800,000 for 30 years so they could buy a $1,000,000 asset, and in return the family will have to pay back the $800,000 over time at an interest rate of, let's say, 3% over 30 years (different from the example we used above). The traditional mortgage would have a principal and interest payment that has to be paid over time; however, you have the choice to pay down the loan faster if desired. Remember that in most cases you use a loan because you do not have enough cash to cover the full cost of the asset (in this case $1,000,000). Let's say, for example, you received an $800,000 net bonus, and you now have the ability to either pay down the 3% mortgage or purchase investment assets that may grow at a rate greater than 3%. Now that you have enough cash to cover the full cost of the mortgage, the question comes down to "Do you believe that the rate at which you borrow (interest rate) will be less than the growth rate of the asset purchased or another like asset?" Assume that short-term rates have risen to roughly 5% while the fixed loan stayed at 3%, the answer is clear: there would be no reason to pay down the mortgage with the excess cash since you could earn roughly 5% on your cash and pay only 3% in interest on the mortgage. Assessing this annually is important as cash interest rates are not guaranteed and may change over time.

Homes and real estate in general tend to increase in value over time. This is a characteristic of using borrowed money to buy a growth asset. When you are borrowing money at a cost (interest rate), it is most beneficial that the asset intended for purchase is growing in value over time to offset the interest paid. We will talk more about bad liabilities in the next section but think about a liability that incurs a cost through debt and the asset purchase goes down in value (car, credit card debit purchases, boats). In these cases, you are paying interest (added cost) for an asset that is also going down in value. If it can be avoided (enough cash on hand), there is no reason to take on debt to buy the particular asset.

Let's look at good liabilities even further as they relate to a company and how a CEO manages a company's balance sheet with his executives. When interest rates were low, many large companies with excessive cash were still borrowing funds. Why would a company borrow money when they have plenty of cash on the balance sheet? The thought process is that the company believes by borrowing money at 4%, for example, the company can use the borrowed funds, invest in the business at a rate better than current interest rates, and make the spread on the borrowed funds. Remember that one of the key terms of the loan is duration, which means that at some point, usually within five years, the company will have to pay back the loan with cash on its balance sheet or go into the market again and borrow funds at current interest rates. With current corporate borrowing rates at roughly 7%, the choice is not as simple, as a rate of 7% could be the forecasted appreciation of the company assets. In this case, the company may actually choose to use excess cash to pay off the loan rather than to refinance the loan at higher rates.

As the CEO of your personal finances, it is important to understand where borrowing rates are, whether it is a mortgage, asset-backed loan, or credit card. In most cases, a mortgage falls into reason number 1 of you do not have enough cash to cover the full cost of the asset.

The biggest risk when dealing with any sort of liability is not being able to cover the loan payments over the particular time frame of the loan. We know that one of the main reasons people use liabilities is to use future cash flow to pay for something now. If cash flow over time ceases and there is an inability to pay down the loan, there is a default or bankruptcy. Whoever lent you the money will be able to most likely take over your purchased asset. When determining how much to borrow (no matter how attractive growth of the asset is relative to the interest rate), making sure that you have the future cash flow to service the debt is the most important item.

Liabilities used to finance income-generating or appreciating assets *may* contribute to long-term wealth when applied thoughtfully and managed prudently. When the expected return on the underlying asset exceeds the cost of borrowing, leverage can enhance an individual's or business's financial position, though outcomes depend on market conditions, cash flow management, and risk. Certain liabilities *may* also offer tax advantages that can improve their overall financial efficiency. In some cases, deductible interest or related expenses can reduce the effective cost of borrowing and support cash flow, depending on applicable tax laws, income levels, and individual circumstances. For example, a mortgage may be used to purchase residential or commercial real estate. Real estate often appreciates over time, providing a potential increase in net worth. Mortgage interest can be tax deductible for homeowners who itemize deductions rather than taking the standard deduction, a benefit that typically applies to higher earners with larger mortgages. Additionally, property taxes and mortgage insurance premiums might also be deductible, further lowering the overall cost. The potential for real estate appreciation, together with possible tax advantages associated with mortgage financing, can make mortgages a useful financial tool for some individuals, depending on their circumstances. The ability to deduct interest and other related expenses may significantly enhance financial management and stability.

Similarly, loans taken to purchase rental properties or commercial real estate can generate rental income and potentially appreciate in value. The interest on these loans is often tax deductible as a business expense if the property is used for rental purposes. This can reduce the effective cost of borrowing and improve cash flow. Investing in real estate with the help of a loan may yield ongoing income and long-term capital gains. The tax benefits associated with real estate investment loans further enhance the financial advantages of this type of liability.

Liabilities that may offer tax benefits can improve financial efficiency by reducing the effective cost of borrowing and supporting cash flow, depending on applicable tax laws and individual circumstances.

Overview of Good Liabilities

A good liability is debt that, when used strategically, can potentially be a great driver of wealth over time. In order for a liability to be "good," it is essential that the money borrowed purchases an asset that appreciates over time and/or produces income that is above and beyond interest paid. The effectiveness of a liability depends on market conditions, borrowing costs, and disciplined financial management, and results may vary. A few examples of good liabilities:

- A mortgage on a home that has a longer duration at an interest rate that is reasonably aligned with the long-term appreciation potential of the property over the time frame of the loan.
- Student loans, depending on the degree of study and interest rate compared to the expected long-term earning potential.

Just like a CEO works with the CFO to determine the use of debt for the company, it is important for you to talk with your CPA and financial advisor to determine the most efficient form of debt when purchasing a home or buying additional investment assets.

BAD LIABILITIES

Bad liabilities are using high-interest debt to buy assets that depreciate or do not generate income; most of the time this includes personal asset purchases. These liabilities, if not managed over time, typically lead to financial strain and do not promote wealth creation.

A bad liability is one that has a relatively high interest rate, with a shorter term, and is used to purchase a tangible asset (car) or an intangible asset that loses value (depreciates) over time.

Credit card debt, for example, is accumulated through purchases made with credit cards, especially when balances are not paid in full each month. Credit cards often have high interest rates, leading to significant interest charges if balances are carried over. Purchases made with credit cards, particularly nonessential items, do not contribute to long-term financial growth. The high cost of interest and the potential for accumulating substantial debt can strain finances, often resulting in a cycle of debt and financial challenges.

Liabilities associated with depreciating assets or high costs often lead to financial strain and do not contribute to long-term financial growth. Managing these liabilities effectively is crucial to avoiding excessive debt and maintaining financial stability.

For instance, loans taken out to purchase new cars that lose value quickly are an example of bad liabilities. New cars typically depreciate rapidly, and the interest on the loan can add up over time. The lack of income generation or appreciation makes this type of liability problematic. Financing depreciating assets with high-interest loans can result in financial strain and negative equity. Managing these liabilities effectively is essential to minimizing their negative impact.

Overview of Bad Liabilities

A bad liability is debt that can ruin wealth and your balance sheet. Unfortunately, most debt that is used today is bad debt; it is money that is borrowed to buy depreciating assets that is not paid off immediately (each month) and grows over time. It's debt that usually carries relatively high interest rates and has a shorter duration. A few examples of bad liabilities:

- Car loans if avoidable—Borrowing money to buy an essential (everyone needs a car) depreciating personal asset. This is not to suggest that loans should never be used to purchase a car, as many individuals do not have the ability to make a large upfront cash purchase. However, when sufficient cash is available, avoiding this type of liability may be the more financially efficient choice.
- Boat loans—Borrowing money to buy a depreciating personal asset. The cost of the loan (interest) is going to add to the total cost of the boat, and future income will be needed to pay down the loan, not the sale of the asset. If you are going to buy a boat, it should be with investment cash that has been earmarked for the goal of owning a boat.
- Credit card debt—The worst kind of debt: built-up debt that is not paid down on a monthly basis to buy assets that do not appreciate over time. Usually, this debt carries very high rates and is essentially making the goods and services that you purchase on your credit card much more expense (since interest is added on).

Just like a CEO works with the CFO to determine the use of debt for the company, it is important for you to talk with your CPA and financial advisor to determine the use of debt for depreciating assets. Sometimes it is unavoidable, but it has to be well thought out, as too much interest cost on a monthly basis can turn a healthy balance sheet into ruins.

CHAPTER 4

SHORT-TERM CASH FLOW MANAGEMENT

"Beware of little expenses; a small leak will sink a great ship."
—Benjamin Franklin

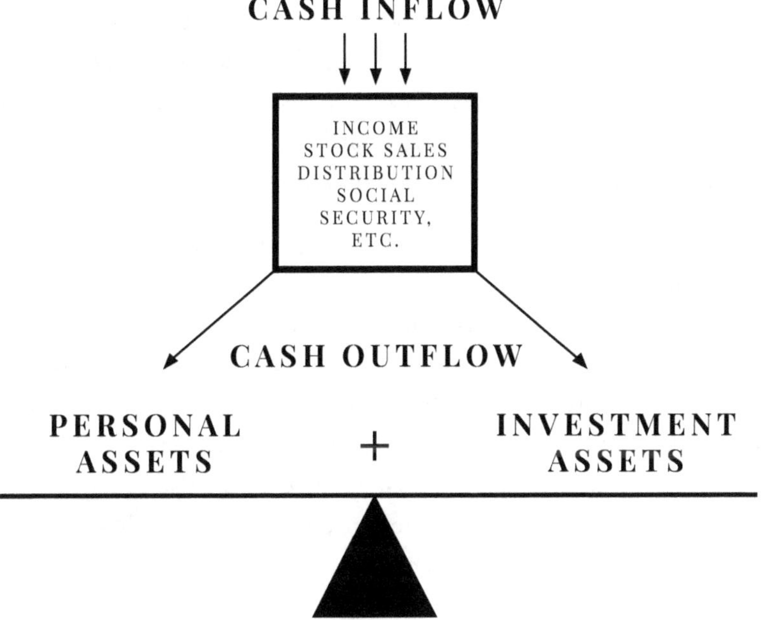

SHORT-TERM CASH FLOW MANAGEMENT is the process of managing the cash you receive from a paycheck, Social Security, or the sale of company stock, for example, into either personal assets (needs and wants) or investment assets (savings). Just like a CEO must decide how to allocate business revenue, you must determine how to allocate your personal cash flow. Effective management of this process is critical to building and preserving wealth.

There are two key components in short-term cash flow management: *cash inflow* and *cash outflow*. We focus on the short-term here, monthly or quarterly management, because these are the moments where momentum is created. Allocating excess cash not used for personal assets to investment assets immediately allows it more time to grow. The long-term side of cash flow management is goal planning, where your investment assets are matched with the duration of future goals (or in the case of a company, the long-term vision of the company); this is covered in the next section on long-term goal planning.

Cash inflow is the cash or currency that enters your checking account. It could be in the form of a salary, bonus, dividends, business income, or inheritance, to name a few. For a business, this simply is revenue. Managing inflow means being intentional about how you earn income and how predictable or variable that income might be over time.

Cash outflow is where the strategic decision-making begins. Once cash enters your checking account, how do you put it to work? Some people spend it all on personal assets. Some save too much into investment assets and forget to enjoy life. Others let it sit in checking, earning little to no interest. All of this is part of the process known as *the Balancing Act.* As CEO of your financial life, your job is to direct that cash strategically by covering your monthly needs (personal assets), then sending the rest to investment accounts (equity, fixed income, opportunistic cash, or alternative investments), where it can grow and eventually replace employment income in the future.

Your checking account typically serves as the central hub for your *cash inflow*. Whether it's a paycheck, a Social Security payment, or other sources of income, nearly all cash is first received into this account. From here, your checking account plays a key role in redirecting cash, *cash outflow*, into either your *investment assets* or your *personal assets*.

Let's now look deeper at each part of the short-term cash flow management process, starting with *cash inflow.*

CASH INFLOW

At its core, cash inflow is simply the generation of cash from a particular source listed below. It's the process of converting your hard work, time, and investment assets into a medium of exchange so you can then buy more personal or investment assets. Cash inflow could also be from inheriting assets if you are the beneficiary. Whether you're a salaried employee, a retiree, or a business owner, the sources of this inflow may vary, but the principles of managing it remain the same.

Generating cash flow in the most efficient way is the foundation of building wealth, and managing the process like a CEO is essential. Without cash inflow, it would be impossible to build long-term wealth.

Cash Inflow Sources for Individuals

- Salary and bonus (conversion of hard work and time)
- Sale of vested stock or options, redirected to your checking account (conversion of hard work and time)
- Sale of an investment asset, redirected to your checking account (sale of investment asset)
- Distributions from a business (conversion of hard work and time)
- Income from a side business (conversion of hard work and time)
- Social Security or pension payments (the result of hard work and time)
- Annuity payments (cash flow from an investment asset)
- Trust distributions (inheritance)
- Liability proceeds (cash flow that needs to be paid back)

- Dividends if used as an income source in retirement (cash flow from an investment asset)
- Interest if used as an income source in retirement (cash flow from an investment asset)
- Rental income if used as a source of income and not reinvesting in properties (cash flow from an investment asset)
- Inheritance, gifts, or donations received (inheritance)
- Alimony
- Disability or unemployment benefits (unfortunate result of the conversion of hard work and time)
- Royalties (conversion of hard work and time)
- Lottery winnings (luck)

For most individuals, their primary source of cash inflow comes from either employment or owning a business. Determining the amount of cash inflow is up to you in terms of what career path you want to choose or how you want to be paid. Knowing your capabilities will direct you in the right path of converting your hard work and time into the medium of exchange of cash to maximize your ability to buy personal and investment assets. You can see above from the various sources that as you increase your investment assets, you also increase your cash inflow over time—not through hard work and time but through cash inflow from investment assets. This is an idea called "earn money while you sleep," whereas the conversion of hard work and time is "time is money." We have only a limited amount of time, so building investment assets to grow cash inflow is crucial.

Every dollar that you allocate to investment assets will either get spent on a personal asset (lifestyle asset) or be given away in the manner that you choose when you set up your legacy plan. Let me repeat that: *every dollar that you allocate to investment assets will either get spent on a personal asset (lifestyle asset) or be given away in the manner that you choose when you set up your legacy plan.*

Why is this? Think about it: when we generate cash inflow from one of the sources above, we then spend a portion on *personal assets* (homes, food, the kids, clothes, travel), and hopefully we save a portion into *investment assets*. The investment assets' role in this cycle is to increase in value over time through growth, dividends, and interest; get monetized (sold) at some point; and then be redirected to a checking account, where they finally get spent on personal assets (rent, mortgage, travel) at the point in your life where you do not have salary cash inflow to fund your lifestyle. This is how people fund their retirement: through the growth of investment assets that are monetized in the future to make up for the lack of income later in life. Otherwise, if you do allocate a portion of your cash inflow to investment assets, you would have to exchange hard work and time versus investment assets to earn cash to fund your lifestyle. Ever hear someone say, "I will have to work until I am 90?" He or she has not reallocated enough cash inflow to investment assets, so they must rely on hard work and time to live, hence working until they are 90. On the flip side of this, if you have guaranteed money for the rest of your life from an outside source that covers all of your personal assets (lifestyle assets), you would never have to save. The reason we save it is to spend the investment asset at a later date on a personal asset or to give away to our beneficiaries or charitable intents based on our legacy plan.

Now let's look at this from a business point of view and review how a CEO thinks about cash inflow. Cash inflow for a business is essential, and without it, there would be no reason for it to exist. It's a vision of all those involved to determine a plan to create cash in a way that helps solve a problem for the customers it serves. Just like your personal financial strategy, a business has many ways to generate inflow. Below is a list of the various sources of cash inflow for a business that a CEO has to strategize on with the executive team:

Cash Inflow Sources for Businesses

- Revenue from sales of a good
- Revenue for services provided

- Dividends and interest from investments that sit on their balance sheet
- Sale of an investment asset that it has been holding on its balance sheet
- Liability proceeds from issuing debt
- Equity proceeds from issuing equity

Most businesses generate the bulk of their cash inflow by selling a product or delivering a service. However, with the right strategy and depending on broader economic conditions, a business can also generate cash by selling some of its investment assets or by raising funds through strategic liabilities (remember good liabilities?).

Overview of Cash Inflow

The cash inflow part of short-term cash flow management is deciding which sources of cash inflow work the best for you now and in the future. It's a function of converting your hard work and time now so you can buy personal and investment assets so that down the road you can rely on investment assets to live and enjoy your time. Just like a CEO of a business, having a strategy for generating cash is important, and having a destination for that cash once it comes in is just as crucial.

CASH OUTFLOW

Cash inflow is money that comes in, usually to your checking account, while cash outflow represents the money that goes out to either personal or investment assets. Just like businesses, individuals have ongoing expenses that consume their cash inflows. However, not all cash outflows are the same. Some are necessary to sustain daily living, while others are directed toward investments that can potentially generate future returns. Managing your cash outflow like a CEO into the right assets is essential to building wealth that will support you in the future. This goes back to **the Balancing Act** that we discussed earlier about managing your cash outflow in the most efficient manner that will cover your personal assets (lifestyle expenses) while also allocating to your investment assets (savings) to build wealth over time.

Cash Outflow Destinations

- Personal expenses for maintaining your lifestyle
    - Mortgage payments (good liability)
    - Potentially other debt payments (hopefully not bad liabilities)
    - Utilities
    - Food
    - Clothes
    - Insurance
    - Health care
    - All the things that pile up in your closet

You get the picture here with the personal expenses. We covered personal assets earlier in the book, and these expenses can vary depending on the lifestyle that you choose. Usually, these expenses do not create long-term wealth and go toward assets that create the lifestyle you choose.

- Investment expenses are focused on building wealth. These may include allocations to:
    - Equity
    - Fixed income
    - Alternative investments
    - Opportunistic cash

Usually, investment expenses do not bring joy with their purchase (some of us enjoy buying them, knowing their role in the financial strategy later in life) but provide a delayed satisfaction down the road, when you have the buying power from these investments to fulfill your lifestyle needs without exchanging your hard work and time. In the last section, when we go over putting all of this together, we will discuss how and where to buy investment assets.

Just like you have the option of allocating cash to personal expenses or investment expenses, a CEO has to manage the business's cash outflow as well to maximize its value. Determining how to best redirect cash inflow to outflow determines the overall growth trajectory for the company.

The CEO, along with the team of executives, has to determine how much to allocate to fixed expenses (similar to personal expenses for you) and to operational expenses (similar to investment assets for you). The allocation of cash to operating expenses is the lifeblood of the business. It is the buying of inventory to sell or the investment in a marketing team to grow a client base. It is the generator of future revenue that will keep the company thriving if managed correctly—just like your investment assets are the generator of future revenue that will supplement your lifestyle when you eventually decide to retire.

In both personal finance and business management, cash management of inflows and outflows requires a high-level decision-making process that will determine the course of the company. Without careful planning, cash outflows can quickly outpace inflows, leading to financial instability. When this occurs, the excess spending will have to be met with a liability to cover the gap in the financing of outflows. This usually leads to a bad liability, which decreases the efficiency of the business.

By understanding the similarities between personal and business cash outflows, you can adopt a more disciplined approach to managing your wealth like a CEO and treating your own cash flow management process like that of a well-run business.

Overview of Cash Outflow

Cash outflow is the second part of short-term cash flow management. It involves strategically deciding where to allocate your incoming cash, toward either personal expenses or investment expenses. Just like a CEO, you must balance lifestyle spending with long-term savings. How much you choose to spend on lifestyle today versus investing for tomorrow will ultimately determine how much income your assets may provide when you're no longer earning a salary.

CHAPTER 5
LONG-TERM GOAL PLANNING

"If you don't know where you are going, you will end up someplace else." —Yogi Berra

ASSETS, LIABILITIES, AND CASH FLOW are the quantitative things in life that are a means to an end. Long-term goal planning is the qualitative part of life that defines what you ultimately want your wealth to provide. It's taking a step back from the day-to-day, planning for the future, and strategically thinking about how you are going to make it happen. Your future goals—ones that are years away—will be bridged with how you effectively allocate your short-term cash flow. Long-term goal planning is managing costs that typically need to be "saved" for and most of the time are not paid for with monthly income. It could take years or decades to pay for them. A few of the more common goals that require planning are listed below.

Long-Term Goals

- Retirement at age X
- Down payment on a first home
- A large-scale home renovation
- A second home
- College education for the kids
- A travel budget every year
- A new car
- A new boat
- Charitable intents

Long-term goals are associated with personal assets, assets that create a lifestyle you want to live. Let's look at a few of the above examples and think about what is really happening when you say you want to retire at 65, for example, or want to buy your first home in five years.

Retirement at 65—Wealth accumulation typically begins when you start your career and often accelerates between ages 40 and 60. During these prime earning years, your main sources of cash inflow are usually salary, bonuses, vested stock, or business distributions. This is the stage when you should be very strategic about where your cash outflows go, either toward personal or investment assets.

Fast-forward to age 65. At this point, a few major shifts usually occur. Your salary, bonus, stock grants, or business distributions often come to an end (retirement), and you begin relying on other sources of cash inflow to maintain your lifestyle. Early retirement years are often active and travel filled, with lifestyle spending peaking in the first decade or two before gradually tapering off in your late 70s and beyond.

At retirement, your primary income sources may now be Social Security or a pension, but in most cases, those alone won't be enough to fully support the lifestyle you've planned for. This is when your investment assets—the ones you spent years building with discipline and that brought little joy to purchase—begin to do their job. They become your new primary source of cash inflow, through the generation of dividends, income, and proceeds from asset sales to cover your personal expenses.

This is the decumulation phase. If there's a thoughtful strategy behind how and when to draw down your investment assets, retirement can be both fulfilling and financially stress free. As you age, the investment assets you've built, depending on the wealth you've accumulated, will either fund personal assets or be passed on, guided by the legacy plan you've put in place.

Remember earlier when I said that every dollar that you allocate to investment assets will either get spent on a personal asset (lifestyle asset) or be given away in the manner that you choose when you set up your legacy plan? This is the time in your life where that truth begins to play out.

College education for a child—College education is a goal that can be viewed as the savings for an investment asset. For example, growing a portion of your wealth to pay for a child's education is essentially an investment in their future earning potential. Ideally, that education leads to a career path that provides a return on the capital invested.

For most families, this $200,000, for example, isn't paid out of annual cash inflow like other personal expenses; it must be built up gradually over many years. As the CEO of your wealth, it's important to treat this as a strategic goal during your planning meetings. That includes deciding how much cash inflow to allocate each year and which types of accounts to hold the investments in.

College planning is a long-term process, and the total cost is a moving target. Tuition, room and board, and other expenses shift over time, and you won't know the exact number until the event gets closer. That's why defining this goal clearly now and committing to a regular cash outflow toward it is essential. Like any major goal, it requires discipline, strategy, and alignment with your other long-term goals.

Just like personal financial strategy, the CEO of a business has to plan for the long term as well. It could be opening a new plant in a different location that could take more than just cash flow to purchase. It could be doubling the staff to meet demand for the product the company sells. It could be acquiring another company. All of these things take additional cash (or debt) to fund, and most of the time they are not funded strictly with operating cash flow.

Think about it. If all of your income goes toward current personal assets like your home, cars, travel, and monthly bills, you will not have excess cash on a monthly or yearly basis to purchase investment assets. Investment assets are the assets that you will sell in the future to pay for all of your long-term-planning items. You have to "save" for college, you have to "save" for a new home down payment, you have to "save" for retirement. Without saving—or, said another way, without reallocating cash inflow to your investment assets—you will never be able to achieve your long-term financial goals, unless there is another form of cash inflow in the future, such as an inheritance. You cannot depend on Social Security alone. This is true for a CEO managing a company. Without a long-term strategy for the strategic vision of the company, the company may cease to exist in the future or be phased out by its competitors.

Overview of Long-Term Goal Planning

Long-term goal planning is defining what you want and need out of life and planning on how you are going to afford it. As you determine your long-term financial goals, there will be a price tag associated with them. Education could cost $200,000 per child, a down payment on a home could be $300,000, retirement could cost $180,000 (a year!). Without strategically reallocating cash inflow to investment assets, the odds of success for meeting your goals will be low.

CHAPTER 6

RISK AND TAX MANAGEMENT

"The essence of investment management is the management of risks, not the management of returns." —Benjamin Graham

BY NOW, you should have a solid understanding of personal and investment assets as well as your good and bad liabilities. You also should have a good understanding of how your balance sheet gets funded through the strategic planning of short-term cash flow management. Finally, you

should know why we invest in the first place—to build wealth that supports your future financial goals and legacy.

Building wealth is only half the equation. Protecting what you've built becomes just as important. Without proper protection, even the most strategic financial plan can veer off course because of an accident, lawsuit, health issue, or unexpected market turn. Managing your wealth like a CEO means you must think like a CRO and a CFO at the same time. Let's look at how to protect both your personal and investment assets and how to increase cash inflow by keeping more of what you earn through tax management.

Protecting Your Personal Assets

Your personal assets make up the foundation of your lifestyle, and as you accumulate these assets over time, they can become a large part of your balance sheet. The same goes for a CEO managing a business; their fixed assets—the assets that keep the business operational—need protection. Without protection, personal assets are vulnerable to unexpected events that could potentially derail a well-thought-out financial plan. Below are ways to protect both your personal assets and the cash inflow that purchases these assets.

Health and dental insurance—Just like a business ensures its key executives because losing them would harm operations, your ability to earn income is your most valuable asset. Health and dental insurance protect against unexpected medical expenses that could force you to dip into savings or derail progress toward financial goals.

Homeowners insurance—Your home is often your largest personal asset, just as office buildings, warehouses, or storefronts are for a business. Protecting it from fire, theft, or natural disasters is critical to maintaining your personal balance sheet. The additional liability coverage also acts like a corporate general liability policy, protecting you if someone is injured on your property.

Renters insurance—Renters insurance is like a business renting commercial space; it needs separate coverage for its own equipment and materials. Your landlord insures the structure, but your belongings and liability exposure are your responsibility, which renters insurance will cover.

Jewelry and personal articles insurance—Just as businesses insure valuable tools, machinery, or inventory with specific riders or endorsements, you may need separate policies for higher-valued personal items. Standard homeowners or renters coverage often isn't enough.

Car insurance—Companies often carry elevated coverage on fleet vehicles to mitigate lawsuit risks. As your personal net worth increases, your liability exposure does too. Your auto policy should scale with your balance sheet, ensuring that you're protected from accidents, medical costs, and lawsuits. Picking the right deductible based on your cash inflow will increase or decrease the premiums on the policy.

Boat insurance—Much like the specialized equipment that companies use, boats introduce unique liability and replacement risks that general policies don't cover. A separate policy should be in place, much like a business would carry separate coverage for critical equipment.

Protecting Your Investment Assets and Cash Inflow

Once your lifestyle is protected, your focus should shift to safeguarding your cash inflow sources and investment assets. These assets are your future. If they're not properly protected, your financial trajectory can be thrown off course.

Umbrella insurance—This policy functions like a corporate excess liability policy. It kicks in after your primary home or auto liability limits are reached. As your net worth grows, so does your exposure. A relatively inexpensive umbrella policy helps protect against large lawsuits that could otherwise put your hard-earned investment assets at risk.

Disability insurance—Just as a company might buy business interruption insurance to replace lost income if operations stop, disability insurance replaces your income if illness or injury prevents you from working.

Use of an LLC for investment assets—Businesses often separate ventures into subsidiaries to limit liability exposure. Similarly, owning a high-risk investment asset, like a rental property, through an LLC can protect your core personal finances from legal or financial claims. Some also use LLCs to manage their assets if they are in a higher-risk profession that is subject to lawsuits—a doctor, for example.

Malpractice insurance—For high-risk professions like physicians, attorneys, and licensed professionals, this is nonnegotiable. It's the personal version of E&O insurance that protects companies. One claim can put your investment assets at risk; malpractice insurance protects this.

Life insurance—If your death would cause financial disruption for your family, then life insurance is your personal version of key person insurance for a business. It can also be used strategically in estate tax management or business succession.

Liquidity insurance (for larger estates)—For large estates, life insurance can serve as a liquidity tool. The primary goal is to help heirs pay estate taxes or equalize inheritance without a forced sale of illiquid assets. It's similar to a business that has credit lines or liquidity reserves to avoid fire sales during market disruptions.

Hedges against concentrated stock positions—If a business relies heavily on one commodity that helps support revenue, it hedges that risk. If your investment assets are concentrated in your company stock, you should do the same. Strategies like collars, prepaid variable forwards, or exchange funds are your hedging tools to protect against volatility while preserving upside and managing tax consequences.

Matching portfolio duration to time—Just as CFOs match the duration of debt obligations with expected cash flows, individuals should align their investment assets (equity, fixed income, alternative investments, and cash) with their cash flow needs. This ensures that liquidity is available when needed, particularly in retirement when the primary cash inflow is dividends, interest, and sale of investment assets.

Long-term care insurance—Extended care needs due to chronic illness or cognitive decline are the equivalent of potentially nonguaranteed liabilities down the road, if at all. A dedicated long-term care policy acts like a corporate pension reserve, absorbing high-cost care expenses so investment assets don't get depleted.

Annuities—Annuities can function like a business's recurring revenue stream, which, if put in place, are predictable, stable, and essential during uncertain times. When structured properly, they reduce longevity risk and provide a steady income floor, much like a business would secure long-term contracts to stabilize cash flow and reduce operational risk.

Increasing Cash Inflow with Tax Efficiency

Protecting your wealth also means minimizing the cost of taxes. Strategic tax management is how you can potentially increase your net cash inflow each year. These techniques require coordination with a CPA and, if appropriate, should be built into your long-term plan.

Tax loss harvesting—Just as a business can offset profits by carrying forward previous losses or writing down underperforming assets, you can sell investments with unrealized losses to offset gains from appreciated positions. This strategy could lower your tax bill without changing your overall investment strategy.

Tax-efficient investing—Companies structure operations across regions to lower tax exposure. You can do the same with your portfolio by using tools like municipal bonds, separately managed accounts (SMAs), direct indexing, 529 plans, and health savings accounts (HSAs). These vehicles help reduce taxable income and improve after-tax returns for some future goals.

Pretax versus Roth analysis—Pretax contributions lower today's tax bill, while Roth contributions aim for long-term tax-free growth of after-tax investment assets. Choosing between the two is like a CFO deciding when to recognize revenue or expenses. The choice depends on your current versus future tax bracket and long-term goals. This is usually unique to each individual.

Mega backdoor Roth—For high-income earners who have an employer 401(k) plan that allows after-tax (non-Roth) contributions and in-service Roth conversions or in-service distributions, the mega backdoor Roth allows you to indirectly contribute after-tax income into a Roth, without being subject to income limits. A mega backdoor Roth is not a direct Roth IRA contribution. This strategy is similar to a business reinvesting surplus profits into high-return R&D initiatives. This advanced strategy can result in future tax-free cash inflow if implemented correctly.

RMD planning—At a certain age, the IRS forces you to begin withdrawing from retirement accounts, whether you need the income or not. Just like a CFO manages the timing of bond maturities or large capital expenses, you must plan ahead to avoid a spike in taxable income.

QCDs (qualified charitable distributions)—When a business donates to charity, it often does so in a tax-advantaged way. A QCD lets you do the same by donating directly from your IRA to satisfy RMDs without triggering income tax. It's especially powerful for retirees who are both charitably inclined and tax aware.

1031 exchanges—Just as companies roll the sale of one asset into another to avoid triggering a tax event, real estate investors can use 1031 exchanges to defer capital gains taxes. This strategy preserves capital and allows the potential for continued portfolio growth.

83(b) elections—For equity compensation, an 83(b) election lets you pay taxes now when the stock is potentially worth less than in the future. It's similar to a company accelerating the recognition of expenses or strategically valuing options at grant to optimize tax impact down the line.

NQDC (nonqualified deferred compensation)—NQDC plans are personal versions of deferred revenue planning where income is pushed into future years when you may be in a lower tax bracket. Not all employees are eligible for this type of plan, however, executives who are eligible to participate use this to smooth cash flow, defer taxes, and control when income is recognized, just like a company carefully times bonuses or contract revenue.

Just like a CEO depends on a chief risk officer to safeguard the company and a chief financial officer to efficiently manage cash flow and reduce tax exposure, you need your own team of professionals to help protect what you've built. Whether it's a financial advisor, CPA, insurance specialist, or estate attorney, these "executives" play critical roles in helping you manage your wealth like a CEO.

Overview of Risk and Tax Management

Risk and tax management are nonnegotiables for protecting all that you have built. Tax management helps ensure that you keep more of what you earn by minimizing unnecessary outflows to the IRS. Risk management helps ensure that what you've built isn't jeopardized by unexpected events. With a risk and tax management plan in place, your wealth has the potential to grow efficiently, predictably, and with far less stress, just like a well-run company.

CHAPTER 7
LEGACY PLANNING

"Only put off until tomorrow what you are willing to die having left undone." —Pablo Picasso

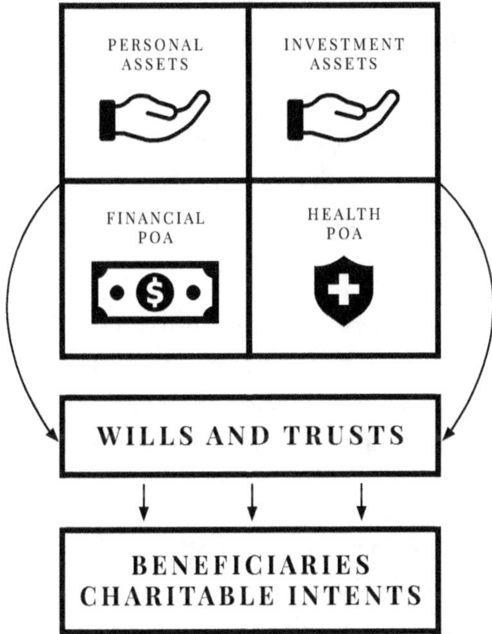

REMEMBER EARLIER when we talked about how every dollar that flows into your balance sheet ultimately gets directed toward a personal asset (a lifestyle expense) or is given away? Legacy planning is how you take control of what happens to your wealth when you're no longer here.

This part of your financial plan is typically built in partnership with an estate planning attorney. Together, you'll map out how your assets are distributed to your beneficiaries according to your wishes. If you don't put this plan in place, the state in which you reside will follow its own intestacy laws to decide who receives what. That process can be slow and expensive and may not reflect what you would have wanted for your hard-earned assets.

Legacy planning is the equivalent of succession planning for a CEO in business. Just like a business can't rely on the same leadership team forever, you, too, need to prepare for what happens when you're no longer managing the day-to-day. CEOs work with their team and board of directors to define succession strategies before something happens, whether that's the death of a key leader or a planned retirement. Here's how each part of your legacy plan mirrors what great business leaders do.

Will—Think of your will as the final directive for how your estate will be dissolved or passed on. Just as an operating agreement outlines what happens if a business is wound down or sold, your will outlines how your personal assets should be distributed and who's responsible for making sure that happens.

Revocable living trust—A living trust is like a continuity plan for your wealth. It allows for the smooth transfer of assets to your beneficiaries without the delay and public process of probate. This is similar to how a business has a continuity plan in place to avoid disruption during leadership transitions.

Durable power of attorney—Appointing a durable power of attorney is like naming a trusted CFO to take over day-to-day financial operations if you're suddenly unable to do so. This person can access accounts, pay bills, and make financial decisions when you can't.

Healthcare power of attorney and living will—These documents are your emergency protocols. In the business world, companies have crisis management plans; so should your personal life. This plan details who makes medical decisions if you can't and what those decisions should be.

Beneficiary designations—Beneficiary designations on retirement accounts, life insurance, and certain investment accounts override your will and transfer assets immediately, similar to how buy-sell agreements determine who gets what in a business sale.

Letter of intent—This is your personal note to those you leave behind. It's not a legal document, but it is an important one. Just like a founder might leave a detailed memo to incoming leadership with guidance and insights, your letter of intent can cover funeral wishes, personal messages, or context around your decisions.

Guardianship designations—If you have minor children, naming guardians is like designating successors to key leadership roles in your organization. You want to ensure that your most important "team members" are in the right hands.

Asset titling review—Just as a CFO regularly reviews how company assets are titled and structured, you need to review how your personal and investment assets are owned. It could be individually, jointly, or in trust. Improper titling can create tax consequences or derail your estate plan.

Charitable giving—Your legacy may include giving back through direct donations, donor-advised funds, foundations, or charitable trusts. Many great companies have a long-lasting impact through some sort of corporate social responsibility planning.

Overview of Legacy Planning

You have built your wealth by exchanging hard work and time for cash inflow, which has shaped your balance sheet of personal and investment assets. While it's never easy to think about your last day, creating a clear legacy plan is a critical part of managing your wealth like a CEO. This plan ensures that your assets are passed on according to your wishes. Legacy planning isn't a one-time event; it requires ongoing collaboration with a trusted estate attorney who understands your evolving goals and can help you make strategic decisions that reflect your values and protect your wealth.

CHAPTER 8

CREATING A FINANCIAL PLAN WITH A UNIFIED "EXECUTIVE" TEAM

"Alone we can do so little; together we can do so much."
—Helen Keller

BY NOW, you should now have a better understanding of assets, liabilities, cash flow, goal planning, risk management, tax management, and legacy planning. How does this all come together so you can manage your wealth like a CEO? Below is an example of a practical plan for working with a team of individuals (key executives) that will cover all of the above so that you can enjoy your life and have confidence in managing your wealth. Whether you are just starting out or well into your career, the below example should help you put together a plan.

The following example is hypothetical and provided for illustrative and educational purposes only. The individuals, assets, liabilities, strategies, and outcomes described are not based on any actual person or situation and are not intended to represent specific financial advice or recommendations. Assumptions regarding investment performance, tax treatment, interest rates, asset appreciation, and strategy effectiveness are subject to change and may differ materially from actual results. Tax laws, plan features, and individual circumstances vary, and strategies discussed may not be suitable for all individuals. Readers should consult their financial, tax, and legal advisors before implementing any strategies described.

Hypothetical Family Situation

- John and Jane are married, both 47
- Sally and Billy are their kids, ages 14 and 16

Personal Assets

- Home: $1,000,000
- Boat: $100,000
- 2 cars (owned): $90,000 in total value
- 1 car (leased): $500 per month
- Noninvestment cash (emergency funds): $100,000
- All the noninvestment related miscellaneous items that are picked up along the way (we all have them)

Investment Assets

- Taxable assets: $2,000,000
- Deferred assets: $1,800,000
- John's unvested XYZ equity: $1,000,000
- John's vested XYZ equity: $500,000

Good Liabilities

- $530,000 30-year mortgage at 3%, which was refinanced in 2021

Bad Liabilities

- Credit card debt: $10,000 at 15%
- Boat loan: $50,000 at 6.5%

Short-Term Cash Management

- $30,000 W-2 net income per month (combined)
- $200,000 annual net cash bonus (combined)
- John receives $100,000 in XYZ equity grants, vesting over four years
- John and Jane both max out their 401(k)s and each have a 3% match
- Each month after personal asset expenses, there is $5,000 left over for investment assets
- Annual bonus, net of taxes, replenishes any drop in the emergency fund, and the rest is saved into investment assets

Long-Term Financial Goals

- Second home with a budget of $1,000,000 in 10 years
- College education for Billy and Sally that could cost about $50,000 per year (estimate)
- Yearly retirement spending of $240,000, starting at Jane's age of 58 (John TBD) and continuing through age 90

Risk and Tax Management Strategies

- Health and dental insurance through John's company
- Homeowners insurance with jewelry insurance
- Car insurance
- Boat insurance
- Umbrella insurance
- Disability insurance for both John and Jane
- Life insurance (term only)
- John has a strategy for managing his concentrated stock position

- John and Jane match their portfolio duration to the time they need the asset
- Tax loss harvesting in their direct indexing portfolio
- John utilizes the mega backdoor Roth contribution through his 401(k) plan
- Jane utilizes her company's nonqualified deferred compensation (NQDC) plan

Legacy Planning Strategies

- Revocable living trust with a pour-over will
- POA for both financial and healthcare needs
- All insurance and deferred assets have beneficiary designations added
- Yearly asset titling review
- Use of a donor-advised fund for charitable intents

Executive Team

- Financial advisor who is a licensed insurance agent
- CPA
- Estate attorney
- Personal lines insurance agent

ASSET AND LIABILITY MANAGEMENT (BALANCE SHEET MANAGEMENT)

Personal Assets—Lifestyle Assets

Below are John and Jane's personal assets, assets that are purchased to run the operations of their family. Remember that these are similar to fixed assets in a business, which are essential to having an operational company.

John and Jane have a *checking account* with about $5,000 that links to their investment accounts. This checking account is the operational account and destination for all of their cash inflow, whether it is their salary, bonus, or proceeds from vested stock. From here they pay all of their operational expenses that are tied to their personal assets. Each month they monitor their net cash in their checking account, and anything left over they transfer to their joint cash account. Their financial advisor will then strategically allocate non-idle cash to their other investment accounts based on prior discussions regarding their financial plan and upcoming cash needs. This process is similar to how a well-run company sweeps excess operating cash into strategic reserves or investment projects.

John and Jane *own two cars outright and lease one vehicle*. The leased vehicle is John's, as he drives only about 8,000 miles per year and likes to have a new car every three years, which is a personal preference. Jane drives well over 20,000 miles per year, so owning her car makes the most sense. Billy's car was Jane's old car that he now uses. When he was ready to drive, Jane purchased a new car and allowed Billy to use her old car. The value of the two cars is $90,000 and declines daily. There is no value for John's car, as it is leased and technically not theirs. John and Jane do not have any loans on their cars, given their higher cash flow and cash reserves. There is no reason for them to have loans, as the added interest cost would just increase the overall long-term costs of the cars.

John and Jane's *home is valued at $1,000,000*; they purchased it for $700,000 in 2018. They have $470,000 of equity in the house, which is the current value ($1,000,000) minus the good liability ($530,000). Originally, they made a $140,000 down payment of investment cash and over time have paid a liability cost and principle paydown on the loan. The amount invested in the home (not including maintenance or other items tied to home ownership) is $170,000 plus the interest costs associated with the loan. In the first few years before the refinance, the yearly interest cost was about $25,000 per year (4.5% on a $560,000 mortgage) but eventually lowered to about $16,000 (3% on a $530,000 mortgage) after the refinance in 2021.

John and Jane have *always wanted a boat.* They had to decide whether they should use a bad liability or buy the $100,000 boat outright. After speaking with their financial advisor, they decided to use a loan for the time being with the intent of paying it down with the next bonus. This allowed them to remain liquid in cash and pay interest for only a year versus the five-year term of the bad liability boat loan.

John and Jane, just like everyone, have *loads of items that are purchased on a monthly basis that create short-term joy* (wants) but over time have little quantitative value. We all know what these are; it could be the things in our storage closet, the things that are on the third shelf in the garage, and also things that hold sentimental qualitative value. They also can be the eleventh pair of shoes, the sixth suit, or the fifteenth shirt or dress that you purchased. These miscellaneous items include all the wants in addition to the needs that are necessary for maintaining a certain lifestyle. While these items may hold qualitative value, they take away from the ability to reallocate cash inflow to your investment assets. Awareness of consumption of "wanted" items is a powerful long-term wealth-building tool.

John and Jane have a *$100,000 emergency fund* in a revocable living trust labeled *"joint cash account."* This cash is managed as efficiently as possible to take advantage of short-term interest rates. If the assets were held in the checking account, the forgone cash inflow from interest would be about $4,000 based on current interest rates. The $100,000 is the amount that they feel comfortable with that will cover their unforeseen expenses rather than dipping into their investment assets, which are earmarked for specific long-term goals. This is similar to how a well-run company keeps a certain amount of cash on the side for unexpected cash flow issues.

Investment Assets—Taxable

Below are the investment accounts that John and Jane set up with their financial advisor using after-tax cash inflow from salary, bonuses, and sale of vested stock. These assets represent the growth engine of their financial enterprise. They are strategically allocated across several revocable living trusts and individual accounts designed to serve different long-term goals.

They have a revocable living trust labeled *"joint core investments."* This account holds a combination of low-cost, tax-efficient ETFs that represent various equity indices, mutual funds for their fixed-income exposure, alternative investment managers for nontraditional exposure, and cash, given that interest rates are around 4%. As they save on a monthly basis, their financial advisor allocates a portion of the incoming cash to this account to be invested in the different asset classes. This is the account that bridges the gap between what they have today versus what they need in the future to pay for their long-term goals.

They have a revocable living trust labeled *"joint direct indexing investments,"* which is managed by a third party to represent the exposure of owning the S&P 500 or a similar index. They own all of the underlying stocks of the index versus owning the one holding of the exchange-traded fund "SPY." The reason for this is that it allows the manager throughout the year to tax-loss harvest and create losses while maintaining market exposure to use at a later date either against income or against the sale of vested stock that has appreciated and is later sold. This is part of the tax management strategy they utilize with the help of their financial advisor and CPA, which we will discuss further in the risk and tax management pillar.

They have two other revocable living trusts labeled *"joint escrow for Billy" and "joint escrow for Sally,"* which are intended to fund some future expenses for Billy and Sally. The accounts are not the children's and remain in the names of John and Jane, just escrowed so they can better plan for potential upcoming expenses for them in the future. The predominant future costs of this account will be toward the unfunded portion of their education and potential financial help of a down payment on their first home. The primary goal is the education portion, and based on the funding levels of their retirement, it is possible they could allocate more funds to these escrow accounts down the road.

John has an individual account with a transfer of death (TOD) to Jane for his account through work. This is where any vested stock from previous grants will initially be held. With the help of his financial advisor, they will determine whether the asset, once vested, should be sold or held for the long term.

Over the past few years, *John implemented a mega backdoor Roth conversion strategy*, which is an advanced method that leverages unused capacity within his 401(k) plan to allow for Roth contributions.

Here's how a mega backdoor Roth conversion works:

- A 401(k) plan allows up to $70,000 per year in total contributions (employee + employer).
- After John maxes out his $23,000 annual deferral and receives his company match, any remaining capacity can be filled with after-tax contributions.
- Since his plan permits in-service withdrawals, those after-tax dollars can then be rolled directly into a Roth IRA, creating tax-free growth potential for life.

Not every employer plan allows this feature, so it's critical to coordinate with the plan administrator, CPA, and financial advisor. This strategy is a staple of corporate-level financial planning applied at the personal level.

John has set up a custodial Roth for Billy, who is 16 and received earned income this year of $2,000. Jane and John contributed the $2,000 to the Roth for Billy to begin his retirement planning at the early age of 16. They plan on doing the same for Sally when she has earned income. Roth IRA contributions can come only from earned income.

John and Jane set up two 529s, one for Billy and one for Sally, that are 75% funded and no longer added to. Any additional savings for college is done through their revocable living trust, labeled as escrow accounts. They are still not 100% sure about the college costs; however, in-state and out-of-state are options for both Billy and Sally. Rather than overfunding the 529s in the event that they go to a lower-priced school, they have optionality with the assets being held in their trust accounts. While 529 plans are highly tax efficient for qualified education expenses, holding additional assets outside the plan provides greater flexibility if education costs differ from expectations.

Investment Assets—Deferred

Below are investment accounts that John and Jane have built through deferred cash inflow. This is money that has not been taxed yet and went directly into their investment account from their income. The three deferred assets that John and Jane have are 401(k)s, IRAs, and a NQDC plan for Jane.

John has a traditional IRA from a 401(k) when he worked at a previous company. After John left his old company, he had the option of keeping the assets in the previous plan, rolling the 401(k) to his new company, or rolling the 401(k) to an IRA, either self-managed or managed by a financial advisor. He also had the ability to roll the 401(k) into a Roth IRA, but given their higher tax bracket, with the help of their CPA and financial advisor he chose not to do this. They ultimately decided to roll the 401(k) to a managed IRA with their financial advisor to have a more dynamic portfolio with equities, fixed income, and alternative investments that matched their risk profile and timeline. If John and Jane were in high-risk professions, such as doctors or lawyers, having their assets in 401(k)s would help them in the event of a lawsuit, as 401(k)s generally have better credit protection than IRAs.

Jane has a traditional IRA that was funded by a previous 401(k) with a former employer. Jane had options similar to John's and also chose to roll her 401(k) into an IRA to have a more dynamic asset allocation managed by a financial advisor.

John has a 401(k) through his current employer where he maxes out his contribution and gets a 3% match from his employer. John has decided to use a target date fund (TDF) for the accumulation phase of his career. This allows him to have a mix of equities and fixed income that automatically adjusts to lower risk over time. When John is ready to retire, he plans on rolling his IRA to his financial advisor to combine all of his deferred assets into one account and manage the assets in a more tactical way during the distribution phase in retirement. Having a selection of equity, fixed income, cash, and alternative investments will allow John and his financial advisor to tactfully sell individual holdings to free up cash over time. Target date funds do not allow this, as when selling a TDF, you have to sell the asset as a whole versus being able to sell equity or fixed income separately, for example. There may be times in heightened volatility that equities should not be sold, or in times of rising markets, it may be best to sell only equities and not fixed income. Having this tactical asset allocation helps with the distribution of investment assets to cash flow in retirement when the assets are ready to be used for purchasing personal assets.

In addition to her 401(k), Jane participates in an *NQDC plan*, which is an executive benefit offered to a select group of employees at her company. This plan allows her to defer a portion of her salary or bonus each year, choosing when she'll receive it in the future and over what time period. After reviewing their long-term tax plan with their financial advisor and CPA, Jane elected to defer a portion of her income for 10 years, with distributions scheduled to begin once she leaves the company and spread over five years. This structure helps smooth out taxable income during retirement, particularly since Jane plans to stop working before John. The deferred income will act as a bridge, potentially keeping their overall tax rate lower during those early retirement years.

The primary goal of an NQDC plan is to defer income while in a higher tax bracket, 37%, for example, and pay taxes later at a potentially lower rate, such as 24%. Of course, this strategy isn't risk free since future tax rates could rise. However, because this plan represents only a portion of their overall wealth, it's a calculated component of a broader, diversified strategy. An added benefit is that Jane's employer provides a partial company match on contributions to the plan, effectively adding "free money" to her future compensation.

Liabilities—Good and Bad

Below are the good and bad liabilities that John and Jane have. As you recall from your reading, good liabilities are typically used to purchase assets that generate income or appreciate overtime. They're strategic in nature and can contribute to long-term financial growth when used correctly. A bad liability, on the other hand, is high-interest debt used to buy assets that depreciate or do not generate income.

John and Jane have one primary good liability, which is their mortgage. When they first purchased their home, mortgage rates were around 4.5%. As rates dropped in 2021, they refinanced into a 30-year mortgage at just 3%. Today, several years later, they are borrowing money for the remaining 26 years at that same fixed 3% rate, while current short-term, risk-free rates sit closer to 4%. At the same time, their home has appreciated nearly 42% since purchased. This is an example of a good liability: borrowing long-term money at a low fixed rate while the underlying asset potentially appreciates at a much higher rate.

John and Jane have two bad liabilities: credit card debt and a boat loan. Credit card debt in general is bad in that the assets purchased are usually personal assets that do not produce income or appreciate and the interest rate is much higher than typical rates. Because of that, John and Jane pay off the card each month so the interest does not accrue. They have always wanted a boat and with the help of their advisor decided to take out a boat loan only for a year. They plan on using it as a one-year bridge so they do not lose liquidity and will pay it off once they get their next bonus payment.

John and Jane are aware of their liabilities and let their good ones run (do not pay them off) and pay down their bad ones as soon as cash is available without letting the duration be too long.

How does an "executive team" help manage a balance sheet?

The balance sheet of a family is the foundation of wealth. It has to be managed like a CEO manages the balance sheet of a business, with efficiency and strategy. John and Jane have *built their balance sheet over time in exchange for their hard work and time*. Working with their financial advisor and knowing all of their available benefits that they have as employees helps them efficiently build their investment assets. Building their balance sheet is only a piece of the puzzle; they have to efficiently manage all of their cash outflow into the right places so they can ultimately plan for their future and determine whether their upcoming costs of education and retirement, for example, are achievable at their desired age. With the help of their financial advisor and CPA, John and Jane have built a solid foundation for their wealth. A few key notes:

- **Checking as their operational account**—They choose to keep only a small amount in their checking account and the balance of their cash in a brokerage account, where they can earn a much higher interest rate than in a checking account.
- **Strategic account structure**—John and Jane choose to have various trusts all titled the same way but with different investment characteristics. Their core investments are low-cost, tax-efficient ETFs, whereas their IRAs have a few mutual funds that are not as tax efficient, which is okay since they are tax deferred accounts. They also choose to have a portion in direct indexing, which allows them to create realized losses throughout the year while maintaining market exposure to offset future capital gains from the portfolio or John's company stock sales.
- **Maximizing employee benefits**—Knowing all that your company has to offer in terms of benefits is important. It allows Jane to take advantage of their NQDC plan and get "free money" from the match they provide as well as defer a portion of her income to later years (not all NQDC plans provide a match, it is important to check with your employer about the features of the plan). Part of the strategy that she discussed with her CPA and financial advisor was how much to defer that would optimize their current tax situation based on their income and equity that vests each year.

They also discussed the ideal timing of the payout based on when Jane plans to retire while John still (potentially) keeps working.

- **Earmarked trusts**—John and Jane have accounts that are in trust name but are earmarked for Billy and Sally in the future to help them with either college or potentially other large-ticket items.
- **Various dedicated college education accounts**—While they are not sure about the total cost of the college education, they have the 529s funded to a level that they are comfortable with while also adding to the Billy and Sally escrow accounts above.
- **Retirement planning for kids**—Since Billy has earned income, they are helping him start his retirement planning early with a Roth IRA.
- **Ongoing reviews and macro outlooks**—During their regular meetings with their financial advisor, they were able to follow lower rates in 2021 and refinance at 3%. Part of their discussions are overall macro environment views that allow them to understand the current economy and act accordingly to better help their financial situation.

Through this structured approach, John and Jane's executive team helps them see their balance sheet as more than a list of numbers. It's a strategic documentation of the result of their hard work and time. It shows where their capital is deployed, how efficiently it's being used, and what adjustments may be needed as their life and goals evolve. And just as a CEO relies on their leadership team to keep the company financially sound, John and Jane rely on their financial team to keep their family enterprise balanced, efficient, and positioned for long-term success.

SHORT-TERM CASH FLOW MANAGEMENT

Cash Inflow

John and Jane have various types of cash inflow that go toward building their personal and investment assets. The cash flow comes from W-2 income, cash bonuses, equity grants, dividends, and interest.

John and Jane earn approximately *$30,000 of net monthly income from their combined W-2 salaries.* This represents the cash that hits their checking account each month after funding their 401(k)s and Jane's NQDC plan. This is their "operating revenue" that must be managed each month to cover living expenses, fund savings goals, and allocate any remaining cash toward future investments.

John and Jane receive about *$200,000 of net cash inflow one time a year through annual bonuses.* When the bonus hits their operational checking account, John and Jane meet with their financial advisor to determine how to best deploy it. Together, they decide how much should flow toward their emergency fund, paying down bad liabilities, funding 529 plans, and adding to taxable investment accounts. This deliberate allocation process mirrors a company's approach to year-end profit distribution, when executive teams decide how much to reinvest versus how much to reserve for upcoming near-term expenses.

John receives about *$100,000 in XYZ equity grants each year as part of his compensation.* While these awards aren't considered cash inflow until the shares vest, they represent a future inflow that must be planned for. Under his company's plan, 25% of the shares vest each year starting in year two. Once vested, the shares are officially his and become part of his available assets in his individual TOD account. At that point, John and his advisor decide whether to sell the vested shares, converting them into cash for redeployment into other personal or investment assets, or to continue holding them as part of his broader portfolio. If the position grows too large relative to their total balance sheet, they strategize on how to diversify gradually while managing taxes.

John and Jane both *max out their 401(k)s and receive a 3% match before the income is taxed.* This inflow skips the operational account and goes directly from income to investment assets without being taxed. John and Jane have the ability to defer their taxes through the pretax 401(k) option, the Roth 401(k) option (saving on an after-tax basis with all future growth and qualified withdrawals completely tax-free), or the after-tax option, which allows only John (Jane does not have this option) to save the cash inflow on an after-tax basis and immediately convert the after-tax funds into a Roth IRA he has with his financial advisor. We will discuss this next in the cash inflow section.

Since John has a more dynamic 401(k) plan that not all companies offer, *he contributes roughly $20,000 per year to his after-tax 401(k) and converts to his Roth IRA* a few times a year. This is a strategy that takes a lot of due diligence with his financial advisor, CPA, and the plan administrator of the 401(k). We will get into the details below.

John and Jane also have cash inflow from their *interest and dividends that they generate from their investment assets.* This cash inflow does not leave the investment side of the balance sheet and gets reinvested each year.

Cash Outflow

Below is how John and Jane determine where the inflow goes once it hits their operational account. Cash outflow is the decision-making process where you allocate a portion of your inflow to personal assets and a portion of your inflow to investment assets—*the Balancing Act.* This entails effectively managing the funding of today's wants and needs versus the funding of tomorrow's long-term goals.

Each month, *John and Jane reallocate $5,000 of their cash inflow to investment assets.* Because of their mortgage, maintenance on the house, and their kids' activities and school costs, their personal assets take a large portion of their cash inflow in order to maintain their lifestyle. After their monthly personal asset costs have been covered, they have about $5,000 left to allocate to their investment assets.

Each year when John and Jane receive a bonus or a portion of John's equity vests, they replenish their emergency fund and cover any bad liabilities. The remaining balance *goes toward investment assets.*

How does an "executive team" help manage short-term cash flow?

Everyone's short-term cash flow management strategy is different. John and Jane have the luxury of many different types of cash inflow, from salary, bonuses, and equity grants. Some may just have a W-2 or 1099 income, whereas some may own a business and get a W-2 salary with business distributions. Either way, having a plan for the capital that comes into your family entity is one of the most important parts of building wealth. Wealth is built through "saving" to your investment assets and to a degree your personal assets. Just like a business needs a strategy for investing capital into operational assets, you, too, should have a plan to allocate the necessary capital to the investment assets that will be your future cash inflow when your employment ends.

With the help of their financial advisor and CPA, John and Jane have built a solid plan for their cash flow management strategy. A few key notes below:

- **Defining target savings**—Based on the financial plan that has been created with their financial advisor, the $5,000 a month plus the bonus inflow is enough to grow their wealth over time for them to retire at their desired ages. This amount was ultimately backed into from the creation of their financial plan. It has changed over the years as their goals evolve and is constantly reviewed as time goes on.
- **Maximizing employer benefits**—Most who participate in a 401(k) with the ability to do mega Roth conversions are unaware that they have that capability. Because John and Jane were aware of all

their benefits as employees, they were able to take advantage of both the after-tax to Roth IRA conversions and the participation in Jane's NQDC plan with the matching component. The mega backdoor Roth and NQDC plans were also discussed with their CPA to better understand their current versus potential future tax rates, which is a key component to building these accounts in a strategic way.

- **Integrating taxable and deferred savings**—While John and Jane's taxable savings of $5,000 compared to their net earnings is on the low end, they have direct cash inflow to their 401(k)s and NQDC plans. Based on their financial plan, they could spend their entire monthly taxable income and save only their bonus and still have a high probability of success for their financial plan.
- **Collaborative planning approach**—Over the years, John and Jane had to strategize with their financial advisor just like a CEO would consult with the executive team regarding how much is needed to outflow into investments to build a successful financial plan. Similarly, a CEO must allocate a portion of the business revenue to the fixed costs (personal assets) to keep the company operating efficiently and employees happy.
- **Targeted savings**—Part of the cash outflow process is deciding where the $5,000 per month of investment asset cash goes. John and Jane allocate a portion of the cash to the escrow accounts they have set up for Billy and Sally for college, and part goes into their core or direct indexing account for their retirement.
- **Retirement planning for their kids**—Billy has a job over the summer and earns $2,000. Because of this, John and Jane can contribute up to $2,000 per year to a custodial Roth for him, capped by yearly limits and earned income.
- **Annual bonus strategy**—Each year when John and Jane receive a bonus, they consult with their financial advisor. They typically replenish their emergency fund and cover bad liabilities if needed

and then allocate the balance to their investment assets. Their primary goal with bonuses is to replenish their emergency fund and contribute to their investment assets. Whatever is left over is used for more personal assets.

LONG-TERM GOAL PLANNING

Long-term goal planning is about defining what you want your wealth to accomplish for you. John and Jane have a clear vision for their future, both for their children and for themselves. Reaching that vision will require a thoughtful exchange of their hard work and time to build the investment assets that will support their goals in the years ahead. With consistent planning and disciplined execution, they are in a strong position to achieve everything they have set out to accomplish.

John and Jane are *looking to purchase a second home in the next 10 years.* The cost of this home will be around $1,000,000 based on their plan, and they have been building their investment assets in their joint core investments account. They may choose to use debt to pay for this in the future, depending on where interest rates are at the time.

John and Jane are *budgeting about $50,000 per year for each child's college education.* They have built investment assets within their 529 accounts, but they have also been saving in separate college escrow accounts in case actual costs are lower than expected. This would allow them to use the escrow funds for their own use versus educational costs for the kids. At this stage, adding more to the 529 plans does not provide as much benefit as it did when the children were younger, when the investment horizon was longer. As time passes and the risk level in the portfolios decreases, the potential for growth also declines. Because of this, the long-term value of the tax deferral becomes less meaningful over time.

John and Jane plan to retire around age 58, although Jane may decide to step away from work a bit earlier than John. Their target spending goal is approximately $240,000 per year, which equates to about $20,000 per month after taxes.

How does an "executive team" help with long-term goal planning?

Every dollar that you allocate to investment assets will either get spent on a personal asset (lifestyle asset) or be given away in the manner that you choose when you set up your legacy plan. All long-term goals are personal in nature since you typically do not set goals to fund your investment accounts themselves. Instead, your investment assets are the drivers of growth that produces future cash inflow once you stop exchanging your time and hard work for income.

With the help of their financial advisor, John and Jane have built a financial plan around their long-term goals. A few key notes below:

- **Future home goal**—John and Jane have a goal to purchase a second home for about $1,000,000 in roughly 10 years. While they could purchase a more expensive home, doing so would require trade-offs such as saving more today by spending less on personal assets, delaying retirement, increasing income, or taking on additional investment risk. After reviewing their financial plan with their advisor, they determined that a $1,000,000 home is achievable based on their current savings rate and spending habits.
- **Matching portfolio duration to time**—Their financial advisor manages their investment assets according to goal duration. For example, the funds earmarked for their future home can be invested more aggressively since that goal is at least 10 years away. In contrast, the funds in the college escrow accounts are managed more conservatively since Billy and Sally's education expenses are approaching soon. Properly managing the sequencing of portfolio withdrawals can help extend the life of their investment assets over time.

- **Retirement spending goal**—Their planned $240,000 annual retirement spending amount is based on their current lifestyle, adjusted for fewer financial obligations as their children become independent. This amount is projected to grow by 1% per year to account for inflation, but it will likely be adjusted over time as their needs evolve.
- **Annual review**—Each year they review their plan and make sure they are still on track with their savings rate and investment assets to cover their intended goals in the future.

Managing your cash inflow and outflow like a CEO is crucial for building lasting wealth. Just as a company's success depends on understanding how money moves through the business, your success depends on knowing how cash enters and leaves your household. By treating your income as revenue and your expenses as strategic investments, you create the discipline to allocate capital toward what matters most. This approach allows you to stay intentional with your spending, maximize your savings rate, and make data-driven decisions about where to direct each dollar. When you manage your wealth with the same structure and awareness as a CEO manages a company, you gain clarity, control, and confidence in your path forward.

RISK AND TAX MANAGEMENT

Managing your wealth like a CEO is more than just building your wealth; it is also about protecting it and making sure you keep more of what you earn. Every successful company has a risk department and CFO to help with tax management. Below are the risk and tax management plans that John and Jane have set up with their financial advisor, insurance agent, and CPA.

John and Jane have comprehensive health and dental coverage through John's employer, along with individual disability policies through their respective employers. Their personal insurance portfolio, which is reviewed annually with their insurance agent, includes a homeowners policy with a jewelry endorsement, auto and boat Insurance, and an umbrella policy that covers up to their current net worth.

John and Jane each maintain a 15-year term life policy designed to replace income in the event of death. These policies help ensure that their family's financial plan can stay on track, even if something unexpected happens.

John has a concentrated stock position from the vested and unvested stock he owns and is owed by his company. Managing this concentration is a key part of their overall risk strategy, helping to control exposure that could otherwise jeopardize their financial stability if his company's stock declines significantly.

John and Jane believe that an important part of risk management is matching the duration of their goals to their risk in their investment assets. Essentially, their time frame of when they need the cash to pay for the goal determines how much risk they're comfortable assuming. Funds earmarked for near-term goals, such as education expenses over the next two to eight years, are invested more conservatively (focus on cash and fixed income with a smaller allocation of equity risk) to reduce volatility. Assets intended for longer-term goals, like purchasing a second home in 10 years or funding retirement over the next 10–40 years, are invested for growth (focus on equity and alternative investments with a smaller allocation of cash and fixed income risk), which can withstand more market fluctuation along the way.

John and Jane use several strategies to enhance tax efficiency within their overall wealth plan. One approach involves managing a portion of their taxable assets through a direct indexing strategy. This allows them to own the individual stocks that make up an index rather than a single index fund. The advantage of this structure is the ability to tax-loss harvest throughout the year, capturing losses on individual positions that can be used to offset future capital gains or reduce taxable income.

With guidance from his CPA, plan administrator at XYZ Corp, and financial advisor, John has the ability to utilize the mega backdoor Roth strategy through his employer. These contributions grow tax free if certain requirements are met, creating a valuable long-term tax-free income source.

Jane contributes to her company's NQDC plan, which functions similarly to a 401(k) but allows for higher deferral limits. This strategy enables her to defer a greater portion of her income into their tax-deferred investment assets, reducing their current taxable income and deferring to a potentially lower tax rate in the future.

How does an "executive team" help with risk and tax management?

With the help of their personal lines insurance agent, CPA, and financial advisor, John and Jane manage their risk and tax efficiency like CEOs. They typically meet with their insurance agent once a year and meet with their CPA and financial advisor several times a year. A few key notes below regarding the strategy that they have for risk and tax management:

- **Health and dental insurance**—John and Jane chose to use John's employer-sponsored healthcare plan because it is the most cost-efficient option and offers a high-deductible health plan (HDHP). This structure allows them to contribute annually to a health savings account (HSA), which grows tax deferred and can be withdrawn tax free for qualified medical expenses in the future. While many people spend their HSA funds each year, John and Jane take a different approach. They pay current medical expenses from regular cash flow and allow their HSA balance to compound tax free over time. By doing so, they're building a future pool of tax-free dollars to use for healthcare costs in retirement.
- **Umbrella insurance**—John and Jane review their personal lines insurance each year to ensure that their coverage keeps pace with their growing net worth. As their assets increase, they typically raise their umbrella liability policy to match their net worth, providing protection in the event that they are found liable for a car accident or an incident that occurs on their property. This additional layer

of insurance sits on top of their home and auto policies, helping safeguard the balance sheet they've worked hard to build.

- **Life insurance**—John and Jane recently renewed their term life insurance policies after reviewing their overall protection needs. The new coverage amounts were determined through a detailed needs analysis conducted with their financial advisor, ensuring that in the event one of them were to pass away, the surviving spouse would have sufficient income replacement to maintain their lifestyle, fund future goals, and protect the family's long-term financial plan.
- **Hedges against concentrated stock positions**—While some have built tremendous wealth through concentrated stock positions, others have lost significant portions of their net worth the same way. As part of their annual review, John's financial advisor evaluates his overall stock concentration in XYZ Corp, which represents roughly 11% of their net worth excluding unvested stock and 28% including it. Since anything above 10%–20% in a single company is generally considered a concentration risk, they carefully review each year's vesting schedule and determine whether action should be taken once shares vest. Because RSUs are typically taxed at the time of vesting, selling shares immediately after vesting typically does not create an additional tax liability if sold near the vested cost basis.
- **Tax-efficient investing**—Direct indexing, the mega backdoor Roth, and the NQDC plan are all part of the tax-efficient strategies John and Jane use beyond their traditional 401(k) contributions. These strategies are not always straightforward to implement and often require additional analysis to determine whether they align with your overall financial plan. Given their strong cash flow and long-term goals, John and Jane are able to take advantage of these opportunities with the coordinated guidance of their CPA and financial advisor.

- **Pretax versus Roth analysis**—Roth conversions will become an important discussion for John and Jane once they retire and potentially move into a lower tax bracket. The strategy behind distributing funds from 401(k)s and IRAs is complex and requires thoughtful coordination between their CPA and financial advisor. The key decision is whether to pay taxes now at a potentially lower rate (through Roth savings) or defer taxes today with the expectation of a lower rate in the future (through pretax accounts). Since John and Jane are currently in a high tax bracket, their plan is to begin converting their retirement accounts to their Roth IRAs strategically in early retirement when their taxable income could be lower. They have structured Jane's NQDC payments to occur during her first five years of retirement, providing income during that period while John continues to work. Once Jane's NQDC payouts end and their household income decreases further, they will begin annual Roth conversions on their 401(k) and IRA accounts, continuing until required minimum distributions (RMDs) begin at age 75. As their income gradually declines (first with Jane's retirement, then with John's), they plan to create taxable income intentionally by staying within a particular tax bracket each year. This approach allows them to convert assets at tax rates equal to or lower than those deferred in currently. It's a complex strategy developed through close collaboration between their CPA and financial advisor, designed to minimize lifetime taxes and maximize flexibility in retirement.

Managing risk and taxes like a CEO is about protecting what you've built and keeping more of what you earn. Just as a successful company protects its assets, diversifies its revenue, and plans intentionally for tax efficiency, you, too, should safeguard your personal balance sheet to reduce any unnecessary drag. By surrounding yourself with an "executive team" of professionals (financial advisor, CPA, and insurance agent), you help ensure that every decision works cohesively toward long-term security. This coordinated approach allows you to mitigate risks before they become threats, manage taxes proactively, and strengthen the foundation of your financial organization.

LEGACY PLANNING

Every dollar that flows into your balance sheet ultimately gets directed toward a personal asset (a lifestyle expense) or is given away. Below is how John and Jane set up their legacy plan with their attorney so that they have control over who gets what when they are gone.

John and Jane created a joint revocable trust, transferring the majority of their taxable assets into it. In addition, they created a pour-over will, which ensures that any assets held outside the trust at the time of their passing are transferred into a family trust, which is established upon the second spouse's death.

John and Jane executed healthcare and financial powers of attorney to protect themselves in the event of incapacity. Each named the other as primary agent, with a corporate trustee appointed to oversee the family trust after both have passed.

John and Jane updated the beneficiary designations on all life insurance and retirement accounts. These assets typically pass directly to named beneficiaries outside of the trust.

John and Jane established a donor-advised fund (DAF), allowing them to make a larger charitable contribution during a high-income year while retaining the flexibility to direct those funds to their desired charities over time. This strategy not only aligns with their philanthropic goals but also enhances the tax efficiency of their overall legacy plan.

How does an "executive team" help with legacy planning?

Just as a CEO relies on a general counsel to guide the company's legal direction, John and Jane depend on their estate attorney and financial advisor to help them navigate the complexities of their legacy plan. Together, they've built a framework that helps ensure that their wealth passes efficiently, privately, and in alignment with their choosing. A few key notes as to how their estate planning came to be:

- **Revocable living trust**—Before creating their estate plan, John and Jane had only a basic will and held all of their taxable assets in joint accounts. If something had happened to both of them, those assets would have gone through probate, leaving their executor burdened with a potentially lengthy and complex process. By establishing a more comprehensive estate plan with revocable trusts, John and Jane built a legacy framework that allows their assets to bypass probate and transfer to their beneficiaries efficiently and based on their wishes with the added guidance of a corporate trustee.
- **Corporate trustee**—John and Jane chose a corporate trustee to manage their estate for their children if they were both to pass away. They didn't want a family member to manage their assets, preferring instead to have a professional trustee act in the best interest of the estate. The corporate trustee will oversee the assets as the children grow older and ensure that the eventual transfer of wealth occurs as planned, according to the ages and milestones outlined in their legacy.
- **Healthcare and financial power of attorney**—John and Jane designated each other as both financial and healthcare power of attorney in the event that one becomes incapacitated. This means that if either were unable to make decisions because of illness or injury, the other would have full authority to manage their financial affairs and make critical medical decisions on their behalf.
- **Charitable giving**—John and Jane established a donor-advised fund and made a significant contribution during a high-income year to front-load their charitable giving. With guidance from their CPA and financial advisor, this strategy allowed them to itemize their charitable deductions in that tax year while maintaining the flexibility to distribute donations to their favorite charities over time. The donor-advised fund functions like a personal foundation

but with far greater efficiency. It offers the same ability to support causes they care about without the administrative work or cost of running a private foundation.

- **Beneficiary designations**—Each year, John and Jane review the beneficiaries listed on their retirement accounts, deferred compensation plans, and life insurance policies. This annual review ensures that their designations remain current with their overall estate plan and reflect any changes in their family or financial situation. By keeping these beneficiary elections up to date, they help ensure that assets pass directly to their intended heirs.

This is an example of how John and Jane, two fictitious people, manage their wealth like CEOs with an executive team. Whether you are a public company employee, a business owner, or just starting out, the above will resonate with you in some way, sometimes in more depth depending on your financial situation.

Managing wealth is not about chasing the next hot investment or allocating your portfolio 70% equity and 30% fixed income, for example. It's about stepping into the role of a CEO. As you've seen throughout this book, the same principles that guide great companies are the ones that can guide you toward a solid personal financial foundation.

The five core areas we've explored are the framework of an operating system for your wealth. When you put them in place, you give yourself the ability to make decisions not from a place of fear or reaction but from a vantage point of strategy and confidence.

Every CEO surrounds themselves with a team of experts but never loses sight of the fact that the ultimate responsibility rests with them. The same is true for you.

As you close this book, the challenge is simple: don't let your financial life drift. You will wake up one day and say, "I wish I had done this or that." Balance sheet management, cash flow planning, risk management, tax management, and legacy planning are the same features that make good or bad companies great. Build your executive team and revisit your strategy often.

Your wealth, when managed like a CEO, can be one of the most powerful tools you'll ever have. Step into the role and lead it well.

www.ingramcontent.com/pod-product-compliance
Lightning Source LLC
LaVergne TN
LVHW010628100826
845148LV00014B/3161

* 9 7 8 0 9 6 0 1 3 4 3 1 1 *